The Church of the
Poor Devil

Other Books by the Author:

The City of the Gods
A Search for God in Time and Memory
The Way of All the Earth
Time and Myth
The Reasons of the Heart

The Church of the Poor Devil

JOHN S. DUNNE

UNIVERSITY OF NOTRE DAME PRESS
Notre Dame, Indiana 46556

Library of Congress Cataloging in Publication Data

Dunne, John S., 1929–
   The Church of the Poor Devil.

   Includes bibliographical references and index.
   1. Poverty (Virtue) 2. Church and the poor.
3. Desire for God. 4. Spiritual life–Catholic authors.
5. Capela de Santo Antonio (Manaus, Brazil) 6. Manaus
(Brazil)–Religious life and customs. 7. Dunne, John S.,
1929–   8. Amazon River–Description and travel.
I. Title.
BV4647.P6D86   1983   208'.80624   83-14548
ISBN 0-268-00746-2 (pbk.)

CONTENTS

PREFACE

I have named this book after a little chapel I found at the end
of a riverboat voyage up the Amazon. Its official name was the
Chapel of Santo Antonio, but its popular name is the Church
of the Poor Devil (*Igreja do Pobre Diabo*). I use it here as an
image of the religion of the poor. It sums up for me an
adventure in passing over from personal religion to the reli-
gion of the poor and coming to a vision of human misery and
the heart's longing.

My adventure began with the riverboat voyage itself where
I encountered people from all the different classes of society
and saw them interact with one another. There were the rich
who were in cabins and the poor who slept in hammocks on
the riverboat, and there were the poorest who lived in huts
along the shore. All together they were an image of human
society. As we voyaged on, day after day, I found myself
entering more and more into the lives of the others, and I saw
others doing it too, people from the hammocks mingling with
people from the cabins, "passing over" I call it. I had written
in my earlier books about passing over to other cultures, to
other lives, to other religions. Here what I was seeing and
doing was passing over from one social class to another. There
was something in it, nevertheless, of all those earlier experi-
ences, for I was passing over from my own culture to that of
the people on the riverboat, from my own life to their lives,
and ultimately, as it turned out, from personal religion, as I
now see my own starting point, to the religion of the poor.

I had begun to think about the religion of the poor while I

was on the riverboat. I saw a hut along the shore with the words over its entrance, "Faith in God" (*Fé em Deus*). I meditated on those words as we voyaged on up the river. It was at the end of our voyage, though, that the image of the religion of the poor crystallized in my mind. It was when I saw the Church of the Poor Devil. All I knew of the little church then was the name. I persuaded a couple of friends from the riverboat to go with me to see it. We learned that it was a chapel of Santo Antonio and that there was a celebration there in June on the feast day of Santo Antonio. I had to come back again two years later, when I had written the first chapter of this book and had started the second, to be at the festival and to find out who the Poor Devil was. I wrote the rest of the book afterward, meditating on what I had seen and learned, hoping to come to an insight into "the sigh of the oppressed," as Marx calls it, "the heart of a heartless world, and the soul of soulless conditions."[1] I invite the reader to join me now, as I reenact my experience of passing over, meditating on the sigh, the heart, and the soul of the poor, hoping to learn from the poor, to let them change our minds and hearts, to join them on their voyage in time.

I come here to a vision of human misery and the heart's longing. These are the two elements in the religion of the poor, human misery—the oppressed creature, the heartless world, the soulless conditions, and the heart's longing—the sigh, the heart, and the soul of the poor. If I ignore or suppress the one element or the other, then passing over to the religion of the poor becomes impossible. If I take the heart's longing to be an illusion, on the one hand, as Marx does, judging religion to be "the opium of the people," then it becomes impossible for me to enter into sympathy with the sigh, the heart, and the soul of the poor. I am left with the conditions under which the poor live, but I have no way of getting inside of the poor themselves. If I take human misery to be something ephemeral, on the other hand, as I am in real danger of doing, coming as I do from an experience of the heart's longing in personal religion, then it becomes impossible for me to understand what the heart's longing means to the poor, living under conditions of poverty and deprivation. If I take both human misery and the heart's longing to be real, as I try to do here, I come to a vision of the human road as a way leading from the human condition to the heart's desire, a way of living in our naked humanity.

It is true, what I am doing here, passing over and coming to a vision, is a work of contemplation more than of action, though it is a kind of contemplation that can be, I hope, the heart and soul of action. Still, passing over to others and coming back to oneself, when it does occur, changes one's relationship with others and with oneself, and when it occurs among a group of people, like those on the riverboat or those in the festival at the Church of the Poor Devil, it is an image of change in human society. It is a way alternative to ways of force and violence. It is the image of a society based on passing over and coming back, on sharing the human essence. It is a changing image much as time is "a changing image of eternity."[2]

I continue here a journey I started in my previous book *The Reasons of the Heart*, "A Journey into Solitude and Back Again into the Human Circle." I am continuing here the journey into the human circle, and I am drawing on the reflections I began there on the heart's longing in solitude. Also that journey into solitude and back again into the human circle is what I am thinking of here when I speak of "personal religion." I am drawing on my earlier books for the way of "passing over," *The City of the Gods* for passing over into cultures by way of death, *A Search for God in Time and Memory* for passing over into lives by way of time, and *The Way of All the Earth* for passing over into religions by way of eternity in time. I am drawing on *Time and Myth* for the distinction between the things of life and the relation to the things. I am drawing mainly, though, on the rich memories of my riverboat voyage and my visits to the Church of the Poor Devil.

I would like to thank Mary Beckman and Tomas Brito, who were with me on my first visit, and Elizabeth Carr, who was with me on my second and more extended visit. Also I would like to thank the scholars at Manaus who helped me in my search for information about the Church of the Poor Devil, especially Geraldo Pinheiro and Mario Ypiranga, and Sister Evelina Trindade, who acted as my interpreter. I would also like to thank the sisters at the Convent of the Precious Blood and the priests at the Redemptorist house for their hospitality when I was in Manaus. Lastly I would like to thank the many friends who offered helpful suggestions and encouragement in the writing, but especially Diego Irarrázaval whose writing (his "Cristo Morado" and later his *Religion del Pobre y Liberacion*)[3] and whose conversation helped me come to realize the importance of the religion of the poor.

The Church of the
Poor Devil

ONE

A Vision of
Good and Evil

A riverboat full of people, rich and poor. A voyage up a great river, from its mouth at the sea toward its sources in the interior of the continent. An image of human life and of the human journey in time. Once I went on a riverboat up the Amazon, from Belém on the coast to Manaus in the interior, a distance of a thousand miles and a voyage of five days.[1]

One scene from that voyage is especially clear and distinct in my memory. It occurred on the first day out on the river. There were two kinds of accommodation on the riverboat: the cabins and the hammocks. The poor had hammocks on the lowest and the middle deck; the rich, and I among them, had cabins on the middle and the upper deck below the sun deck. On that first day we sailed past many small huts along the riverside where poor people lived off of the river and the jungle. As we passed, women and children from these huts came out in small canoes to meet us. People in the riverboat began throwing clothes out into the river, and those in the canoes would paddle quickly to retrieve them. In the riverboat people were shouting and cheering and laughing. In the canoes people were not laughing but looking up at us with a kind of wonder, though they would smile when they succeeded in retrieving the clothes. Someone beside me said, "Do you see who is throwing the clothes?" Then I looked and saw that the clothes were being thrown from the lower decks. It was the people from the hammocks who were throwing the clothes and doing most of the shouting and cheering and laughing. The people from the cabins were only watching.

It was as if the people from the hammocks shared a life with the people in the canoes, while the people from the cabins stood outside of that life. As we went on, nevertheless, the people from the hammocks began to mix with the people from the cabins. At first they were timid about coming to the upper deck—they would come to the bar, buy a soft drink and quickly drink it while looking about them, and then hurry back down to the lower decks. After a while, though, they began to become bolder and take chairs on the upper deck or sit at tables there with one another and play dominoes. I began to meet people from the hammocks and talk with them. Our usual life began to dissolve with all its distinctions, and we began to become one with one another in our companionship on the voyage. I began to feel that I was being admitted to the richness of a life that I had only observed when I saw them throwing clothes to the people in the canoes. As we journeyed toward the sources of the river, we seemed to be journeying also toward the sources of human life.

I saw a vision of good and evil there on the Amazon. There was an eclipse of the human essence in the class distinctions with which we began our voyage. Then, as the voyage went on and the class distinctions began to dissolve, there was a shining forth of the human essence, a disclosure of the richness of human life. "The human essence is no abstraction inherent in each single individual," Marx has said. "In its reality it is the ensemble of the social relations."[2] Or is it the other way around? Is the human essence present in the individual but eclipsed by the ensemble of the social relations? Does it shine forth in the individual when the social relations are transformed?

A Voyage to the Sources of Life

On the riverboat I saw the richness of human life both in individuals and in people together. I suppose the human essence, therefore, was present in individuals and also in the relations of people with one another. It was present in a man carrying his child on his shoulders, in an adolescent girl from the hammocks smiling shyly at a young woman from the cabins, in two men sitting at table playing dominoes, in two young women walking one behind the other and laughing, in a woman from the hammocks sitting on the deck floor among men, in a man with a telescopic camera taking shots of the jungle, in the bartender opening beers and soft drinks, in two boys wrestling with each other on the deck floor. *What is the human essence?* Surely Marx is right when he says it is "no abstraction inherent in each single individual." It is something too rich to be an abstraction, and yet it is present in each single individual and every one of them reveals some aspect of its fullness.

I saw something else, however, when I looked at people's faces to see if they were happy. Looking at people's faces in this way is something I had done as an adolescent boy, gazing at face after face, searching for happiness, hoping to find someone who was happy and to learn the secret. This time I saw something more like a poverty than a richness of life. There was a grim look on the face of the man carrying the child, for instance, a hardness contrasting with the softness of the child, although there was the softness and the tenderness of him actually carrying the child on his shoulders. He was a man from the hammocks. "In its reality," Marx says of the human essence, "it is the ensemble of the social relations." There is indeed a reality about the ensemble of the social relations, real enough to block the way to happiness, to condemn this man from the hammocks to a desperate struggle for existence. Still, it seems to me, the ensemble of the social relations is not itself the human essence. That is why there is hope.

We are shaped by the ensemble of the social relations, according to Marx, but it is we ourselves who shape the social relations. "Men are products of circumstances," he says, but "it is men that change circumstances."[3] The people from the hammocks and the people from the cabins were divided by their circumstances, but they were able by mingling with one another to dissolve, at least in image, the class distinctions that divided them. Are our circumstances then the sources of our life? Or are the sources of life within us? It seemed to me on our riverboat voyage that we were discovering the sources of life within ourselves. As we voyaged to the sources of the Amazon, the many tributaries that issue into it, we were coming also to the sources of our own life, the inner resources that make us capable of changing our circumstances. We were on the way, though we never carried through, to the ultimate sources of the river. We went only as far as Manaus where the greatest of the tributaries, the Rio Negro, issues into the Amazon. Similarly, in our journey to the sources of human life, we went only so far as to discover the richness of human existence. We were traveling, though, in the direction of the ultimate sources of our life.

If I were to complete our voyage now in thought and come to the ultimate sources of human life, I would come upon the source of evil as well as that of good. Like Marlow in Conrad's story of a riverboat voyage up the Congo, I would come to the "heart of darkness." But if evil is "an eclipse of the human essence," as I am conceiving it, and not the human essence itself, I would come ultimately to good, to the heart of light. Let me try to carry the voyage through, all the way to the heart of light and of darkness.

I hope "to make contact," as Dag Hammarskjold says, "with that in human nature which is common to all men, indestructible, and upon which the future has to be built."[4] I hope to make contact, that is, with the human essence. On a voyage to the sources of life, a voyage together like ours, there is an experience of "passing over," I call it, of people entering into each other's lives. Here is where I hope to discover the human essence. Is it possible for a person from one social class to understand one from another, for someone from the hammocks to understand one from the cabins, for example, or for someone from the cabins to understand one from the hammocks? Is it possible for a person from one society to understand one from another, for someone like me from North America to understand one who lives on the Amazon or for someone there to understand me?

"No, it is impossible," Marlow says when he is about to tell of his voyage up the Congo. "It is impossible to convey the life-sensation of any given epoch of one's existence—that which makes its truth, its meaning—its subtle and penetrating essence."[5] Yet that is just what I would like to convey about our voyage up the Amazon, "the life-sensation," "that which makes its truth, its meaning—its subtle and penetrating essence." I do believe it is possible, nevertheless, for "its subtle and penetrating essence" is the human essence; it is what we have in common. "It is impossible," Marlow says. "We live, as we dream—alone." Yet if we do live alone as we dream, then our aloneness itself is something we have in common, something we can convey to one another and understand. Let me take our aloneness as my starting point in "passing over."

There is such a thing as an aloneness without privacy. That is the experience of aloneness I found among the people from the hammocks. Privacy is freedom from the company or observation of others. There was little privacy in the hammocks. The people there seemed accustomed to living always in the company of others and being always observed by others. At the same time there was an aloneness I could see in them, the basic aloneness of human beings who have their own hopes and fears, their own dreams and daydreams, their own thoughts and choices. Music was playing constantly on the ship's phonograph, popular music from the interior of Brazil. It was the music of the people from the hammocks and was enough to crowd out any feelings or thoughts of their own and fill their mind with those of the collectivity. Still, they did have feelings and thoughts of their own. They were accustomed to the music as they were to company and observation. Some had an aloofness about them, as they stood among others, not attending to the company of the others or the eyes of others upon them, not listening to the music, but looking at someone or something in the distance. Their aloofness was an aloneness, I could see, and it was not taken away or even diminished by their lack of privacy. It was a removal in feeling and interest, a distance from the others who were thronging about them.

I found another experience of aloneness among the people from the cabins. It was the aloneness of people who have the experience of privacy, who are able to live without the constant company and observation of others, who are even able to travel, as these people did, at great distances from their dwelling place and from those who are most connected with them. A person who enjoys privacy can experience a loneliness, a longing for companionship, for the presence of others. There is a special word for this in Portuguese, *saudade*. It means "longing," especially longing for those who are absent. One of the people from the cabins, a young woman, spoke to me of this word. She was feeling the absence of her lover, far away in São Paulo, the young man she was soon to marry. She was lonely and very conscious of her loneliness and had a well-chosen word for it. That suggests to me that although it is a basic human feeling, something that can be shared by all human beings, *saudade* is a very conscious kind of loneliness and longing. It even has a history: it is the theme of the Fado (fate), a kind of song that was first sung in Brazil by those who had come from Portugal, then carried back to Portugal itself, and now regarded as the traditional folk song of Portugal.

I brought still another experience of aloneness with me from North America. It too was a loneliness, a longing for companionship, for the presence of others, but not so much for particular others who were absent. Rather it was an indefinite longing for intimacy, for relatedness, a feeling of being alone and wanting to be unalone. "Not only does democracy make every man forget his ancestors, but it hides his descendants and separates his contemporaries from him," de Tocqueville says of democracy in North America. "It throws him back forever upon himself alone and threatens in the end to confine him entirely within the solitude of his own heart."⁶ The loneliness I brought with me was just this feeling of being separated from all others, of being thrown back upon myself and confined within the solitude of my own heart. Thus it was not like *saudade*, a loneliness based on connection with others, a longing for persons with whom one is connected. Rather it was a loneliness based on disconnection, and so it was an indefinite longing for some kind of connection.

Privacy and lack of privacy, connection and lack of connection, all these situations existed on the riverboat. All of them belong to "the ensemble of the social relations." Aloneness, on the other hand, belongs to the human essence present in each single individual. If I wish to understand the poor and their lack of privacy, or to understand the longing that comes from connection with others, I must take my stand in aloneness. No doubt, my starting point is the most alone conceivable, privacy and lack of connection. Still, there is an aloneness, as I observed, that can exist in connection, like that of the people from the cabins, and one that can exist in the lack of privacy, like that of the people from the hammocks. If I pass over, therefore, from my own aloneness to theirs, I begin to understand how my aloneness is not simply privacy and lack of connection. I can see a way of saying "No man is an island." If my aloneness were unshared, were simply privacy and lack of connection, I would be an island. As it is, I realize I am "a piece of the continent, a part of the main."[7] My aloneness is shared. It is that of the continent, the main.

Say I pass over to the people from the hammocks, going over from my privacy to their existence without privacy. The worst thing about being poor, it has been said, is that "it makes it almost impossible for one to be alone."[8] It makes it almost impossible, that is, for one to have privacy. As I see what it is like to live without privacy, I realize I want to be alone. Before this point I had been thinking I was lonely and wanted the company of others, but the sight of people crowded together in the hammocks makes me realize how aloneness is something desirable. Yet when I see also how the people from the hammocks can be alone in the midst of their lack of privacy, how in spite of everything they have their own thoughts and feelings, I realize we have aloneness in common. The person from the hammocks can know as well as I do what it is to live in the solitude of one's heart. There is a difference between us; I have privacy and the person from the hammocks does not. Yet there is common ground: we both live in the solitude of our heart. Really we live in the same solitude. It is as if we lived in the same wilderness, the same desert or the same forest. We can meet there.

Say I pass over also to the people from the cabins, going over from my lack of connection to their connection with others. We also can meet in solitude. The people from the cabins, or the ones I came to know, seemed to live out of their human ties. When I saw how much human ties could mean, how intensely a person could long for the loved one who is absent, I began to realize how indefinite my own longing had been. I had been longing simply to be unalone, to find someone or something. It was not that I had no human ties. Rather I had not been living out of the human ties I did have. The loneliness I brought with me from North America, the loneliness of being thrown back upon oneself and confined within the solitude of one's heart, I began to see or I see now as I reflect upon it all, was not due to a lack of human ties but to a disregard of the ties that actually exist.

Here are two thoughts then, the thought of being alone and living out of the human essence within oneself and the thought of being unalone and living out of human ties. What if I put these two thoughts together? Robert Louis Stevenson speaks in "An Apology for Idlers" of those who have "not one thought to rub against another, while they wait for the train."[9] That image of rubbing one thought against another is a helpful one here. If I rub one of these thoughts against the other, a spark is kindled, an insight into the human essence. It is that we are sources of life to one another and yet we have the source of life within ourselves. Or better, we are sources of life to one another *because* we have the source of life within ourselves. It would be those who have not yet discovered the source of life within themselves who have "not one thought to rub against another, while they wait for the train."

If the human essence were present only in man and woman together, say, and not in man by himself and woman by herself, then we would be sources of life to one another but we would not have the source of life within ourselves. So it would be also if the human essence were present only in "the ensemble of the social relations" and not in each single individual. As soon as I contemplate the idea of the human essence being present in man and woman together, I must admit, I can see there must be some truth in it. Freud's vision, if we were to translate it into these terms, would be just this, that man and woman are sources of life to one another but do not have the source within themselves apart from one another. It is a vision of need: a human being is never whole but is always a being in need. Marx's vision is parallel: the human essence is present in human beings together, not in the small togetherness of man and woman, to be sure, but in the large togetherness of human society.

My experience of our voyage together on the riverboat points in the same direction, to a presence of the human essence in human beings together, in man and woman together, in all of us together. My experience of passing over, though, taking aloneness as my starting point, going over to the aloneness without privacy among the people from the hammocks and to the experience of absence and longing among the people from the cabins, points to a presence of the human essence in each single individual.

Presence is the key element in the experience. We are sources of life to one another because when we are together something becomes present among us, a richness of human life, what I have been calling "the human essence." The presence in all of us together, though, begins to be felt only when we begin to pass over and to enter into one another's lives. That is the way it happened on the riverboat. At first, the human essence was eclipsed by the separations among us, especially by that between the people from the cabins and those from the hammocks. For me there was a further separation, between me and both those classes of people on the riverboat. The separations began to break down then as we began to enter into one another's lives. We began each to share more fully in the human essence that had been divided up, as it were, among us. To share life with others and lack privacy like the people from the hammocks, to have privacy and stand outside the life of others like the people from the cabins, to lack human ties or not live out of the human ties one does have like me, is to have something of the richness of human life and to lack something of it. When we began to enter into one another's lives, we began to come into a kind of fullness of life. It is then that the human essence began to shine forth among us. It is then that its presence among us began to be felt.

Its presence makes me think of the presence of God; its eclipse and its shining forth make me think of the eclipse of

God and the shining forth of God. I think of that now as I reflect upon it and try to complete our voyage in thought, carrying it through to the ultimate sources of life. At the time, however, while I was on the riverboat, I thought only of the richness of human existence. Our voyage, it is true, seemed *meant* somehow, even at the time, and to that extent God seemed to be at work in it. What I encountered on the voyage, nevertheless, seemed to be something human. As I carry it through now in thought, therefore, shall I look for the source of human life in God?

Marx says of Feuerbach that he "resolves the religious essence into the human essence,"[10] and Marx himself goes on to resolve the human essence into "the ensemble of the social relations." My experience, our voyage together and our entering into one another's lives, is leading me in the opposite direction, from the social relations to the human essence and its presence among us. Shall I take the further step now, from the human essence to the religious essence? As I understand it, "the religious essence" is the image of God in human beings. It is what is spoken of in Genesis, "So God created man in his own image, in the image of God he created him; male and female he created them."[11] It is present, as the words imply, in man and woman. Feuerbach has it the other way around, that man has created God in his own image, in the image of man he has created him. Thus Feuerbach "resolves the religious essence into the human essence." But he never says what the human essence is. If I do the reverse, resolving the human essence into the religious essence, I am saying that human beings are in the image of God, that the human essence is a relationship with God, that we have the source of life within ourselves because God is in us.

Is there an inexhaustible source of life within us? That is the question, put in terms of our voyage to the sources of life. If our voyage seemed *meant*, it was because of the richness of life we discovered on it. But is the richness of life inexhaustible? A person might draw the opposite conclusion from an experience of boredom. "In the absence of conflict, of contending interests, of anguish and agitation," Herbert Read has Olivero say in *The Green Child*, "I had induced into my environment a moral flaccidity, a fatness of living, an ease and a torpor which had now produced in me an inevitable ferment."[12] Instead of "a richness of life" there is in boredom "a fatness of living." The "inevitable ferment" that boredom produces, however, the dissatisfaction that arises from an exhausted life, seems very similar to the indefinite longing for someone or something, the loneliness that comes from a lack of connection with others. That longing and loneliness, I found on our voyage, instead of being an ending, can be a starting point for passing over to others, for discovering a richness of life that has been hidden by the boredom and exhaustion of our social relations.

I heard a story while I was at Belém, before our voyage began, about a Spanish caravel at the mouth of the Amazon. It was a parable of exhaustion and inexhaustible life. It took place in the days of the great voyages of exploration.[13] The sailors aboard the caravel were dying of thirst. The caravel was floating in the wide expanse of waters at the mouth of the river. The sailors were dying of thirst, that is, while they were floating, without knowing it, in fresh water. We are dying of thirst, the story seems to say, because we believe we have already exhausted the sources of our life, while in reality we are floating in a life that is inexhaustible. There is a darkness here, an unknowing and a dying, and there is a richness that is hidden, an inexhaustible life.

The Heart of Light and Darkness

An eclipse of the human essence is sometimes spectacular like an eclipse of the sun. That happens when it takes a massively destructive form such as mass murder or mass suicide. Mostly, though, it is not spectacular and is something you can see only if you are aware of the richness that is hidden, the inexhaustible life. At first I didn't realize I was seeing an eclipse of the human essence in the class distinctions on the riverboat. We lived apart from one another, the rich in the cabins and the poor in the hammocks, and we ate apart from one another, the people from the cabins sitting at table in a dining room and the people from the hammocks lining up to receive their food on plates. It was only after a while, as the class distinctions began to dissolve, as I began to perceive the richness of life, that I knew there had been an eclipse. Our living apart from one another, our eating apart from one another, all these things, I saw, were expressive of our separation from one another. It was a partial eclipse, to be sure, if you compare it with the total eclipse that occurs in more spectacular instances, in suicidal and murderous forms of human evil. Yet it seemed to partake of the evil, of the separation from one another that is at the heart of murder and suicide.

Is separation then the "heart of darkness"? Surely it is our separation from one another that hides what we have in common, the human essence. Conrad's *Heart of Darkness* is a tale in which "we live, as we dream—alone." It is the story of a riverboat voyage up the Congo in which Marlow, the narrator, encounters what he calls "a choice of nightmares."[14] One nightmare is made up of the soulless agents of a trading company and their soulless grubbing for ivory. It is a nightmare of soullessness. The other is made up of the wilderness itself and its inhabitants and Kurtz who has gone in there among them to find ivory but has come to be worshipped by them. It is a nightmare of soul, of worship and being worshipped. Marlow prefers the nightmare of soul to that of soullessness, but he tells Kurtz, "You will be lost—utterly lost," and he hears Kurtz's last words, "The horror! The horror!"[15]

There is a separation in a nightmare of soul, an isolation

from one's fellow human beings that has become conscious, but there is an even greater separation in a nightmare of soullessness, an isolation that has remained unconscious and thus has become all the more unfeeling. Soul is a depth of life and of feeling; it is our capacity for inexhaustible life. Soullessness, on the other hand, is more an absence than a presence; it is a lack of all greatness or nobleness of mind or feeling. Our separation from one another on our riverboat voyage up the Amazon was at first unconscious, the eclipse of the human essence was at first observed, and so it partook of the unconscious and unfeeling quality of a nightmare of soullessness. My seeing the eclipse, however, as I became aware of the life hidden by our separation from one another, partook of the feeling and the awakening that can occur in a nightmare of soul. It was an awakening to good and evil. There was "a moral victory,"[16] Marlow says, in that cry, "The horror! The horror!" There was a moral victory for me too, I think, in seeing the eclipse of the human essence. It was not simply a vision of evil. It was a vision of good and evil, of good eclipsed by evil, and ultimately of good emerging.

Soul, according to Conrad's story, may be "tenebrous and passionate"; it may be "as translucently pure as a cliff of crystal"; it may be "mad," knowing "no restraint, no faith, and no fear, yet struggling blindly with itself."[17] Let me trace our passage from soullessness to soul, as we entered into one another's lives on our voyage together. It will lead, I am hoping, straight into the heart of light and of darkness.

We were a "ship of fools,"[18] an image of human society in disarray, as long as we lived in our separation from one another. There was soul, it is true, in the shared life of the people from the hammocks; there was soul also in the *saudade* of the people from the cabins; there was soul too in my indefinite longing. But there was soullessness in our separation. It is not the feeling of separation that is soulless. "Loneliness is not the sickness unto death,"[19] Dag Hammarskjold says in a diary where "loneliness" is the most frequent word. Loneliness is the feeling of separation and, as feeling, belongs to soul. Separation is soulless when it is unfeeling, when it is not even lonely. An image of soullessness in Conrad's story is the manager of the trading company who "inspired neither love nor fear, nor even respect." "He inspired uneasiness," Marlow says. "That was it! Uneasiness."[20] That was the initial feeling among us, between the people from the cabins and those from the hammocks, not a whole and entire feeling like love or fear or respect, but something nearer to a lack of feeling or the obscure beginnings of a feeling, uneasiness.

Uneasiness is a restlessness. As it grows, it can become more and more a feeling. It can turn into loneliness. It can also turn into conflict. It arises out of our separation from one another and can lead toward greater and greater separation, toward death. After saying, "Loneliness is not the sickness unto death," Hammarskjold goes on to say, "No, but can it be cured except by death?" When he says "death," his thoughts go to suicide. But thoughts can also go to murder. Here is where the vision of evil arises. You are able to see the depth of our separation. At the same time, the feeling for separation enables you to recognize, when you see it, our capacity for sharing life. For the feeling becomes a longing for union, for inexhaustible life. Here is where the vision of good arises.

As I entered into the lives of the people from the hammocks and saw how they were able to share life with one another, I saw an image of what was missing in me and in the people from the cabins. I saw an image of soul. It was "tenebrous and passionate." Or so it appeared when I first encountered it. Their shared life seemed "tenebrous" to me, mysterious, because I did not yet participate in it myself, did not know what it was to live without privacy and constantly share everything with everyone else. Actually the sharing was imposed on them by their lack of privacy. Still, there was a spontaneity about their sharing, a willingness, a cheerfulness, as appeared when they were throwing the clothes to the people in the canoes amid shouting and cheering and laughing. Their sharing with one another came from within themselves, it seemed to me, even though it was imposed by their circumstances. Thus their life seemed "passionate," full of feeling like their music, and I was attracted to it, wanted to participate in it, believed I would discover in it what was lacking in my own more separate existence.

When it came to actually sharing life with them, I found we had only common things to share, sitting together on deck in the shade, exchanging a few words, a smile, a wave, telling each other our names, where we came from, where we were going. Somehow with their manifold origin, Portuguese, African, American Indian, I expected stranger things of them, and maybe they expected stranger things of me, coming from North America. But there were only common things— ordinary things, that is, and things we had in common, the two meanings of "common." It was the sharing itself, I suppose, that was significant, not the things we shared. There was no gain in things, only in relatedness. Indeed, that was the gain I sought, to go from separation to sharing, from unrelatedness to relatedness. That was their secret too, to share life however common.

I found what I sought also among the people from the cabins, a relatedness less inclusive than the sharing of life, it is true, but all the more intense and absorbing. I saw how *saudade*, the longing that arises out of human ties, if carried far enough, can make a soul. I saw how "a soul as translucently pure as a cliff of crystal" is possible. Purity of heart can come about through a negative process of renunciation, by giving up all the many things that can divide your heart among them. Or it can come about instead by an affirmative process of intensification, by giving yourself ever more fully to a relatedness. That intensification can come about in *saudade*, I saw, as a person becomes more and more absorbed in longing, more and more involved in living in a relationship. Here again the contrast appears between things and relatedness. Things are absent: you are longing for someone or something that is absent. Relatedness is present: its presence becomes more and more intense as you become more and more single-minded and single-hearted. You begin to love "with all your heart, and with all your soul, and with all your might."[21]

Is it good, though, to love anyone or anything other than God "with all your heart, and with all your soul, and with all your might"? Actually, to love that way, I believe, is always to love God. When the loved one is absent and everything else drops away, there is nothing left but the relationship itself. Then, if you are in it heart and soul, it can become transparently a relationship with God—I think of Dante seeing Beatrice in paradise, seeing her smile at him and then following her gaze toward God.[22] It is similar if you give yourself to the kind of relatedness I found among the people from the hammocks, a relationship that is inclusive rather than exclusive, a sharing of life. That too, if you are in it heart and soul, can become transparently a relationship with God—I think of a hut I saw along the Amazon with a sign over the door, "Faith in God" (*Fé em Deus*).

Indeed, if you are in it heart and soul, an indefinite longing for someone or something, like the loneliness I brought with me from North America, can become transparently a longing for God.[23] It is when it fails to become transparent, it seems, that a soul can become "mad" with longing, knowing "no restraint, no faith, and no fear, yet struggling blindly with itself." Longing fails to become transparent when there is no passing over, no entering into the lives of others. Then it appears to be simply an expression of our utter aloneness. There is "no restraint, no faith, and no fear" because there is no one other than ourselves to reckon with, to believe in, to fear, and yet there is still longing, "struggling blindly with itself." We seem trapped in some kind of lonely darkness, and our longing becomes "like the cry of some evil and lonely creature."[24] It is true, "loneliness is not the sickness unto death," but when there is no passing over, no entering into the lives of others, then the longing in loneliness becomes something dark at work in our lives, something "evil and lonely," a nightmare of soul, a "heart of darkness."

There is a light, I found, that shines forth in that darkness of longing when you pass over to the lives of others. You see a relatedness, something of what you are longing for, as I saw in the sharing of life and in the longing that arises out of absence. Not only that, but passing over is itself a relatedness, and you can actually enter into the lives of others. An indefinite longing, for all its darkness, enables you to enter into the many shapes of human relatedness, while itself remaining indefinite, unfulfilled, a longing only God can satisfy. For someone like me, coming out of a loneliness that throws you back upon yourself and threatens to confine you within the solitude of your own heart, it becomes essential to enter into the darkness of longing, to find there a basis for passing over, to find there a longing for God.

"Even for the most perfect," Yeats says in *A Vision*, "there is a time of pain, a passage through a vision, where evil reveals itself in its final meaning."[25] Yeats is thinking here of figures like Christ. Not only for someone coming out of an unrelatedness, if he is right, but even for one who is whole-hearted and whole-souled, it can become essential to enter into the darkness of the human heart. It is "a time of pain" when you enter there, he is saying, "a passage through a vision," like our passage from soullessness to soul, a time when you come to a vision of good and evil, "where evil reveals itself in its final meaning." But what is "its final meaning"? Our separation from one another? If evil is really an eclipse of the human essence, as I have been saying, then its meaning will not be final. It will be rather an eclipse of meaning.

A sharing of life that is imposed by a lack of privacy, a

longing arising out of human ties that are exclusive, a longing that has become indefinite, these are all phases of partial eclipse, like phases of the moon, a crescent moon, a half moon, a gibbous moon, where the full moon would be to love "with all your heart, and with all your soul, and with all your might." There is relatedness and unrelatedness, therefore, meaning and eclipse of meaning. If there is meaning in relatedness, there is eclipse of meaning in unrelatedness. Our unrelatedness is our separation from one another. It is not a harmless lack of meaning, to be sure, but something potentially destructive, murderous and suicidal, whether it is feeling or unfeeling, more so perhaps when it is unfeeling, for then the unrelatedness is greater. To see "the Vision of Evil," according to Yeats, is to "conceive of the world as a continual conflict."[26] It is to see, I would say, the conflict arising out of our separation from one another, but ultimately it is to see the separation itself, to see the unrelatedness that is at the heart of all destruction.

Suicide is at the heart of murder, I think, a separation from ourselves at the heart of our separation from one another. The disrelation is between ourselves and our lot in life. According to Yeats in *A Vision*, the vision of evil has taken two classic forms, one of "the unworthiness of man's lot to man" and another of "the unworthiness of man to his lot."[27] If I look at the people from the hammocks, the eclipse of the human essence I saw on our riverboat voyage took that first form, an "unworthiness of man's lot to man." Their lack of privacy was expressive of their entire condition in life. "The worst of poverty—today at any rate—the most galling and most difficult thing to bear, is that it makes it almost impossible for one to be alone," Theodor Haecker says in *Journal in the Night*. "Neither at work, nor at rest, neither abroad nor at home, neither waking nor sleeping, neither in health, nor—what a torture—in sickness."[28]

If I look rather at the people from the cabins and at myself, the eclipse of the human essence took that other form, an "unworthiness of man to his lot." We lived in privacy and in longing. We were alone and we wished to be unalone. It was as if we did not realize we were on a voyage together. We were each on a personal journey—certainly I was on a personal journey. What we lacked, what I lacked, between being alone and wanting to be unalone, was a heart-and-soul willingness to be on a personal journey—not a *will* to go alone that excludes companionship but a *willingness* to go alone that welcomes companions. When you are willing to be on a personal journey, you step into your own aloneness, say Yes to it, become one with it. You find "a way a lone a last a loved a long the riverrun."[29] At the same time, you find that the way "a long the riverrun" is a way for everyone, that you have companions on the journey, that we are on a voyage together. A time like that came for me on the riverboat, a moment of vision, a moment of conversion.

I saw in that moment how our voyage on the riverboat was an image of the human journey in time, how the "ship of fools," as Katherine Anne Porter says, is a "simple almost universal image of the ship of this world on its voyage to eternity" and how "I am a passenger on that ship."[30] That for me was a vision of good. There was a passing over to others and a coming back to myself, a realization that we were on a voyage together and a willingness to be on that voyage myself. It was a glimpse of the human essence. Passing over to others reveals how we are sources of life to one another; coming back to yourself reveals how we have the source of life within ourselves. If our separation from one another, "the world as a continual conflict," is a darkness, then our separation from ourselves, the disrelation between ourselves and our lot, brings us to the "heart of darkness." So too, if our relatedness with one another on our journey together in time, the "simple almost universal image of the ship of this world on its voyage to eternity," is a light, then our conscious and willing participation in the journey, the Yes in that avowal, "I am a passenger on that ship," brings us to the heart of light.

When I speak of the "heart of light," I mean the human essence, really "the religious essence," our capacity for a relationship with God. When you are on an exclusively personal journey, as I was at first, as the people from the cabins were, you may find the essence in yourself, but to no avail for longing and for loneliness. You go alone "into the gaze and silence of the Lord."[31] When you pass over to others, when you give up privacy or do not even have privacy, like the people from the hammocks, you can find the essence in others, but again to no avail. It is in others, not in you. When you come back to yourself from passing over, though, you find it in yourself again, and now to some avail. For now you know the essence can be shared without a loss or lessening. You know it is a source of inexhaustible life.

When Plato speaks of the vision of good, he says "the good is not essence, but far exceeds essence in dignity and power."[32] That is his most emphatic statement about "the good," and here I am, speaking instead of "the human essence" and yet speaking also of "inexhaustible life." If you conceive the human essence, as I do, to be our capacity for a relationship with God, then "a glimpse of the human essence" is a glimpse of something that points beyond itself. *God has no essence*, I can say, as Aquinas was willing to say,[33] meaning God is not confined to our relationship with God. There is something in a vision of good that "is not essence," I can say therefore, "but far exceeds essence in dignity and power." A vision of good, nevertheless, is for me "a glimpse of the human essence," a discovery of relationship or of capacity for relationship. Just to see our voyage as an image of the human journey in time was for me a vision of good. Where I see something that "is not essence, but far exceeds essence" is in life being inexhaustible. Here is where I come upon infinite richness of existence, where I see how "God has no essence."

There is inexhaustible life in a relationship with God, and every human relationship, if I am right, whether it is an inclusive sharing of life or an exclusive longing arising out of absence or even an indefinite longing for someone or something, becomes transparently a relationship with God when you are in it heart and soul. Following a human relationship to God is like following a river to its sources. If you follow the Amazon to its sources, you come upon many tributaries, and finally you come to a point where you don't know which is the tributary and which is the river. After you pass the point we came to, Manaus where the Rio Negro flows into the Amazon, the river changes its name, from the Amazon to the Solimões. Ultimately, if you follow it one way, you come to a lake high in the Andes. If you follow it another way, you come to a mountain spring in southern Peru.

A human relationship too, if you follow it to God, changes its name. One relationship leads into another, if you pass over, and each one leads differently to God. A sharing of life can lead, as I saw on the hut along the Amazon, to a "Faith in God." A longing arising out of absence can lead, like Dante's longing for Beatrice, to a "love that moves the sun and the other stars."[34] An indefinite longing, because it is full of undefined hope and fear, can lead to a "living Dread whose fountains yet flow mercy."[35]

It is Cain in William Vaughn Moody's unfinished play, *The Death of Eve*, who says, "Thou living Dread whose fountains yet flow mercy!" Eve and her son Cain, as the only act of the play ends, are on their way "into the gaze and silence of the Lord," searching for the lost garden of paradise where human beings once walked with God. Our voyage to the sources of life, to the heart of light and of darkness, was a journey in that same direction. It too was unfinished, like Moody's play, and can only be completed in thought, as I have been trying to do, by following out the lines of the relationships in which we were living. There is a clue in the title, *The Death of Eve*. If following a human relationship to God is like following a river to its sources, the actual course of human life is more like the river's own flowing to its mouth at the sea, a passing into death. A voyage to the sources of life goes against the current of life itself.

There is an answer here to my original question, "What is the human essence?" Somehow the human essence seems to emerge in going against the flow of life toward death. It emerges in coming into touch with the inexhaustible source of life. "Men perish," Alcmaeon, an early Greek philosopher, said, "because they cannot join the beginning to the end."[36] We die, he seems to be saying, because we don't know how to find the inexhaustible source from which our life is flowing. The human essence, let us say, is a capacity for joining the beginning to the end, a capacity for a relationship with God. Joining the beginning to the end would mean going on a voyage to the sources of life.

An eclipse of the human essence would consist then in not knowing or not being able to join the beginning to the end. There is death in that, as Alcmaeon says, murder and suicide, we have seen, or rather the unrelatedness we have seen at the heart of all destruction. There is death the other way too, like the death of Eve, even though we come to the inexhaustible source of life, but it is a death that is full of life. If an unrelatedness among human beings is an eclipse of the human essence, then a relatedness that becomes transparently a relationship with God is a shining forth of the human essence. That is the true utopia, it seems to me, not simply a classless society but one in which human beings relate to one another out of a fullness rather than an emptiness.

TWO

The Church
of the Poor Devil

At the end of our voyage up the Amazon we came to Manaus, and there I came upon another image of human life and of the human condition. It was the Church of the Poor Devil (*Igreja do Pobre Diabo*), a tiny church, really a kind of tall chapel. At first I thought it might have something to do with devil worship, and I felt some uneasiness about even going to see it, but when I looked through the cracks around the locked doors, I could see it was simply a Catholic chapel with an altar, a crucifix, and a statue of Santo Antonio. I could see the wax of many candles spilled on the threshold and the pavement all around. Who then, I wondered, is the Poor Devil?

According to one story the Poor Devil was the poor workingman who built the chapel.[1] According to another the Poor Devil was a woman, "a tall, fat, and masculine mulatta" who used to beg and who finally had the chapel built with the alms she collected.[2] According to another the Poor Devil was a beggarman who collected a fortune in alms but then gave it all away to the needy.[3] According to another the Poor Devil is Santo Antonio himself.[4] What is the true story? I was in Manaus again two years after my first visit, this time to be at the festival of Santo Antonio in June when the chapel is actually open, and I found a metal plaque had been set on the door of the chapel with the inscription:

CAPELA DE SANTO ANTÔNIO
CONSTRUIDA POR CORDOLINA ROSA
DE VITERBO DOADA À DIOCESE A
28—11—1897
"IGREJA DO POBRE DIABO"
FUNDAÇÃO CULTURAL DO AMAZONAS

"Chapel of Santo Antonio, constructed by Cordolina Rosa de Viterbo, given to the Diocese on November 28, 1897, 'Church of the Poor Devil,' Cultural Foundation of Amazonas." I was able to get a copy of the deed in which Cordolina gave the little chapel to the Diocese (though I found the deed was dated October, rather than November 28, 1897). I learned that Cordolina was indeed a mulatta, that she couldn't read and write (the deed mentions this), that she lived with a man named Antônio José da Costa, a Portuguese who had a cabaret and who used to call himself "the Poor Devil," and that after his death and their deathbed marriage, Cordolina used to call herself "the Poor Devil."[5]

There are three principal characters in the story, therefore, the woman Cordolina, the man Antonio, and the saint, Santo Antonio. But there is also a fourth, I learned further on, a black woman who is called the Mother of the Saint (*Mãe de Santo*) and who presides over African rites that are connected somehow with the Church of the Poor Devil. During Cordolina's time the Mother of the Saint was a woman named Joana. At the present time it is a woman named Zulmira. I had a feeling of the uncanny, of dread and fascination, at the prospect of meeting Zulmira just as I did at the prospect of seeing the Church of the Poor Devil when I knew only its name and thought it might have to do with devil worship. What is more, I was to meet her at night—I felt like Saul going to meet the witch of Endor. When I actually met her, though, my sense of dread began to fade, just as it did when I actually saw the little chapel. There was a quiet friendliness about her and a feeling of warmth that was very reassuring. Yet she showed me something that filled me with wonder. She led me into a *barracão*, a kind of barn with several rooms, and in one of them she showed me a large and lighted replica of the Church of the Poor Devil filled with statues of saints corresponding, as she told me, name by name, to African gods and goddesses.

My experience of going from something uncanny to something human and yet full of wonder, when I saw the little chapel, when I met Zulmira, as I reflect on it now in retrospect, seems an experience of "passing over." I was passing over from my personal religion to the religion of the poor. Let me try to reenact that experience now in slow motion and see if I can come to some kind of insight. "Religion is the sigh of the oppressed creature," Marx says, "the heart of a heartless world, and the soul of soulless conditions."[6] Let me see if I can gain some insight into that sigh, that heart, and that soul.

The Heart's Desire

Knowing only its name, I had approached the Church of the Poor Devil with some misgiving. I thought anything was possible on the Amazon. When I actually saw the little chapel, though, I had an impression rather of purity and simplicity. It was very small, "four meters wide by eight meters and twenty centimeters long," as the deed says, and made "of brick and stone, roofed with tile and floored with mosaic." It was painted white with blue trimmings. The gray foundation of masonry reached to about a meter or so above the ground in front, and the white upper structure was done in stucco. The doorway was tall, about four meters, with a trefoil arch; the doors were made of iron rods, painted silver, with curling ironwork in the arch; and there was a porthole window over the arch. There were two small white towers with pinnacles on either side of the facade; and there was a gable roof with crockets, and a white cross on top. I could see the "golden section" in the proportion of the width of the chapel to its height. Somehow the little chapel seemed to have its own beauty, beyond all ulterior purposes. It seemed an expression of heart's desire.

What is the heart's desire? Is every house, every design, an expression of heart's desire, or does its expression have to be something like the Church of the Poor Devil? Consider the Theatre of the Amazon built at Manaus during the rubber boom at the turn of the century, at the same time as the Church of the Poor Devil. The great theatre, many times the size of the little chapel, is the expression of a moment of exaltation, a time of power and glory. Its use and disuse over the years reflect the boom-and-bust of an economy. To be an expression of heart's desire, let me propose, a work has to have three qualities:

    (A) It must be a labor of love
    (B) It must express a relationship with God
    (C) It must be on a human scale

It must be a labor of love, though it need not be done for merely personal use or enjoyment, to be an actual work of heart's desire. It must express a relationship with God, though it need not be a church, to express the full reach of the human heart. And it must be on a human scale, proportionate to the human body, though it need not be small, to be in accord with the limits of human life.

"My house is practical. I thank you, as I might thank Railway engineers, or the Telephone service. You have not touched my heart," the architect Le Corbusier says. "But suppose that walls rise towards heaven in such a way that I am moved."[7] A work cannot touch the heart, cannot move me, unless it is a work of the heart, unless it comes from being moved. It must be a labor of love. But if it is able to touch the heart, able to move me, it will be because "walls rise towards heaven." It must express a relationship with God. And if "walls rise towards heaven in such a way that I am moved," it will be because they have some proportion in human eyes, because the house is proportionate to the human body. It must be on a human scale—"and this work is on his own scale, to his own proportion, comfortable for him, to his measure," Le Corbusier says of man building. "It is on the human scale. It is in harmony with him: that is the main point."[8] There is a relation, that is, between heart's desire and human needs. If it is possible to meet human needs without moving the heart, as in the house that is only "practical," then human needs must be differentiated from heart's desire. But if the work of the heart must be "on the human scale" and "in harmony" with the human being, then heart's desire must also be integrated somehow with human needs.

Needs and heart's desire go together in a labor of love. There is a happiness in a labor of love like the Church of the Poor Devil, although that name, the Poor Devil (*o Pobre Diabo*), means "the poor wretch" in Portuguese just as it does in English and tells of needs that are unfulfilled. If I enter into this labor of love, reenacting it in thought, I am in for some kind of reconstruction myself, going from the complexity of meeting my needs to the simplicity of following my heart's desire. Let me see if I can discover here the link between the human and the spiritual, the thread running through all the needs, the true desire of the human heart.

To understand what is going on when a person builds a chapel for a saint would be to understand much about human existence, both about human needs and about heart's desire. There are the needs that appear in the recourse to the saint in prayer, and there is the heart's desire that appears in the building of the chapel itself. Is it possible, I wonder, to understand popular religion from a standpoint of unbelief? I think of

Freud calling it "an illusion"[9] and Marx calling it "the opium of the people."[10] Is is possible to understand it even from a standpoint of personal religion? I think of Kierkegaard calling it "childish Christianity."[11] My own starting point is one of personal religion, but my task here, as I see it, is to pass over to the standpoint of popular religion, to enter so far into the feeling of popular religion that it no longer seems an illusion or an opium or a childishness, to find in myself the needs that are being expressed there in prayer and to let myself be carried by the feeling and expression of need into the feeling and expression of heart's desire.

According to the story of Cordolina, as I heard it recounted (on a tape made by an old black woman who knew her),[12] she made a *promessa* to Santo Antonio, a promise that if he would do something for her, she would build a chapel for him. What she was asking of Santo Antonio is not known. It may have had to do with Antonio, the man she had been living with, or it may have had to do with her son, who was also called Antonio. It may have had something to do with her marriage, for Santo Antonio is the matchmaker in Brazil, and young women make *promessas* to him in this form, "If he (the one I love) marries me, I promise you. . . ."[13] Whatever it was, it had to do with some need of hers. The expression of need, the appeal to the saint, goes before the expression of heart's desire, the building of the chapel. "If you will help me in my need, I will build a chapel for you." What I am calling "the expression of heart's desire" is seen as something desired by the saint rather than by the person in need. It comes through to others, nevertheless, as a following of heart's desire—to those who saw Cordolina's energy in carrying out her promise, to those like me who simply see the finished chapel.

If I enter into my own needs, I gather from the story, I will come upon my heart's desire not as my own desire but as the desire of some power greater than myself to which I am having recourse. That seems very true to the experience of trying to do God's will. Say I have been trying to find hap-

piness by meeting my needs and have found my life becoming
more and more complicated because my needs are manifold
and no one thing seems able to satisfy them all. My will seems
to be "falling asunder," as Yeats says, and I am beginning to
realize that I can find happiness only by some kind of
"simplification through intensity."[14] When I try to move
toward "willing one thing," as in Kierkegaard's formula,
"Purity of heart is to will one thing,"[15] I seem to be moving
toward doing the will of God rather than my own will. There
is some further moment then when I realize that the will of
God is not alien to me, that in willing one thing, in doing the
will of God, I am happy, I am following my own heart's
desire. That comes about in actually carrying out what I
perceive to be the will of God. It will have come about for
Cordolina, I can imagine, in actually carrying out her promise
to Santo Antonio, in actually planning and building her
chapel.

I think of Le Corbusier building the Chapel at Ronchamp.
He is asked to build on a hill above Ronchamp where there
has been worship from time immemorial, where the ruins still
exist of a chapel destroyed by artillery fire during the Second
World War. As he sits on the hill, the idea of the chapel comes
to him with its concave and convex walls and roof. "There is
no practicable road to bring transport to the top of the hill,"
he discovers. "Consequently I shall have to put up with sand
and cement. Probably the stones from the ruin, cracked by
frost and calcined by fire would do for fill but not for load
bearing." But these limiting conditions themselves tell him
how the work is to be done. "An idea crystallizes," he says:
"Here, in these conditions at the top of a lonely hill, here we
must have just one all-embracing craft, an integrated team, a
know-how, composed of men, up there on the hill, free and
masters of their craft."[16]

An idea crystallizes also for me, when I am trying to go
from the complexity of meeting my needs to the simplicity of

doing the will of God. I am doing something analogous to the making of a *promessa*: I am turning over the task of meeting my needs to God while taking on myself the task of fulfilling God's will. When I do that I come upon the limiting conditions under which I must work, like the conditions Le Corbusier finds at the top of the hill. I can find within those conditions, nevertheless, the freedom or scope to fulfill the new task I have taken upon myself. In fact, those very limits outline for me what I am to do. An image emerges, like the image of the chapel and how it is to be built. It is an image of my life, for instance the image of my life as a journey with God. "My life is a journey in time," I once wrote in a diary, "and God is my companion on the way." Indeed a chapel is itself the image of a life. It can be "an imitation of grace flying up and up from the mud,"[17] as the Elephant Man (John Merrick) called the church he used to spend his time modeling. He labored under the limiting conditions of an affliction that had deformed his head and most of his body, and his whole life, as he worked on his church, became a "flying up and up from the mud." Whatever it is, the image expresses the movement of heart's desire, and when I contemplate it, I realize God's will and my own deepest longing are one.

"An imitation of grace" is what Merrick sees in Saint Phillip's Church, and "my imitation of an imitation" is what he sees in the model he is making of the church. "But even in that is heaven to me," he says. It is the expression of his heart's desire, that is, arising out of the limiting conditions of his affliction. If I look at the Church of the Poor Devil that way, as "an imitation of grace," not indeed as a pictorial representation but simply as an expression of the working of grace, I can see the movement of heart's desire there too. Or better, I can see the sort of thing that happens in a *promessa*, an interchange between heart's desire and human needs.

What are a person's needs? One kind of need, let me propose, is that recognized by Marx and linked with what I have been calling "a labor of love." It is the need that appears in the story of the poor workingman building the chapel with his own hands, the need for a life arising out of his own inalienable labor, and it encompasses a whole gamut of particular needs, from the necessities of life to the need for self-realization.[18] Its fulfillment is suggested in Le Corbusier's words, "here, in these conditions at the top of a lonely hill, here we must have just one all-embracing craft, an integrated team, a know-how, composed of men, up there on the hill, free and masters of their craft." Another kind of need is linked with what I have been calling "a relationship with God." It has to do with the events of life, what happens to a person, and it is the need Cordolina will have been concerned about in making and keeping a promise to Santo Antonio, that the right thing would happen to her Antonio or to her son or to herself. Its fulfillment is suggested in Roethke's line, "The right thing happens to the happy man."[19] A third kind of need is linked with what I have been calling "a human scale." It is the need for a world that is human, that is proportionate to the human body, the need Cordolina will have been trying to meet in the actual design of the chapel, that Le Corbusier was trying to meet in his system of proportions based on the "golden section" and the human stature. It is the unfulfilled need Merrick was struggling with as the limiting condition of his life.

What then is the heart's desire? If something like the Church of the Poor Devil is its true expression, then it has something to do with God as well as with human existence. But is that its true expression? "Religion is only the illusory sun about which man revolves," Marx says, "so long as he does not revolve about himself."[20] If I think of Antonio calling himself "the Poor Devil," if I think of Cordolina calling herself "the Poor Devil," Marx seems right, the Poor Devil "does not revolve about himself." And if I think of the saint as the recourse of all poor devils, then it seems "religion is only the illusory sun about which man revolves." But if I think of Cordolina building her chapel, of Le Corbusier and his workers "free and masters of their craft" building the Chapel at Ronchamp, of Merrick building his imitation of "an imitation of grace flying up and up from the mud," then it seems the Poor Devil is like the earth, turning on its own axis while orbiting around the sun. Even the saint then, the recourse of all poor devils, no longer seems an "illusory sun" but somehow the image of a sun that is true to heart's desire. And that is the heart's desire, I begin to think, to be like the earth, turning on the axis of human existence while orbiting around the sun that is God's existence.

If I try to enter into the needs and heart's desire of others, the question arises for me too: what are my needs? What is my heart's desire? What is it for me to turn on my own axis? And what is it for me to orbit around the sun? Coming out of a culture that separates one person from another and "throws him back forever upon himself alone and threatens in the end to confine him entirely within the solitude of his own heart,"[21] my feeling for human needs and heart's desire is conditioned to some degree by the experience of living within the solitude of my own heart.

I have an experience of complexity in trying to meet my needs, trying to escape from the solitude of my own heart, going from one person to another, from one situation to another, an experience of "dispersal," as Yeats calls it, and "enforced self-realization."[22] When I differentiate between heart's desire and the need for self-realization, on the other hand, I begin to find my way to simplicity. There is something pure and simple about being willing to live in the solitude of my own heart. It means following my heart's desire. For when I become willing to live in that solitude I find God there, I find what I could never find when I was unwilling to be there, and I find other human beings as well, I enter the solitude of their hearts by entering that of my own. To be able to orbit around the sun I have to be willing to turn on my own axis, to live in the solitude of my own heart, but to be able to turn on my own axis I have to be willing to orbit around the sun, to leave aside the many directions I have not taken and give myself heart and soul to the journey with God.

A labor of love is able to express the heart's desire while at the same time, you would think, meeting the need for self-realization. When I pass over into Cordolina's labor of love, though, or Le Corbusier's or Merrick's, coming from my own experience of living in the solitude of my own heart, I see how a labor of love is actually a symbolic integration of life. It does express heart's desire but the self-realization it brings is symbolic. It leaves Merrick with his affliction; it leaves Le Corbusier saying, "Come what may";[23] it leaves Cordolina calling herself "the Poor Devil." If everything a person did were a labor of love, then self-realization would be achieved. As it is, unfulfilled needs are like boundary conditions to heart's desire.

A "boundary condition" in physics is the vanishing of a quantity at infinity or its remaining finite at infinity, when otherwise it would become infinite at infinity. A "boundary condition" as I mean it here is something analogous. If I recognize no boundary conditions, my pursuit of happiness can become infinite, stopping at nothing, but if "I am in need" to me is like "I must someday die," then I have to find an expression of heart's desire that is compatible with being in need, that is compatible for me with living in the solitude of my own heart. It is possible, I learn from the experience of a labor of love, to express my heart's desire without fulfilling all my needs. On the other hand, the expression of heart's desire, while not itself fulfilling needs, is an image of their fulfillment. A labor of love, I can see then, is a symbolic integration of life, and it points to an actual integration that is yet to come, to an Omega of some kind, a happy ending, a consummation of human affairs.

Meanwhile the symbolic integration of life takes shape out of circumstances. "An idea crystallizes: here, in these conditions at the top of a lonely hill . . . ," as Le Corbusier says, and so it supposes that the circumstances are somehow full of meaning. The boundary conditions themselves, that is, the unfulfilled needs, instead of being only barriers to heart's desire, are signs pointing the way. What I am calling "boundary conditions" are comparable to what Karl Jaspers calls "boundary situations": "I am in need" is comparable to "I am always in situations," "I cannot live without struggling and suffering," "I cannot avoid guilt," and "I must die."[24] Like the boundary situations in which I find myself, the boundary conditions limiting my happiness at a given time are occasions of insight. When my life opens up before me at the prospect of death, I may come to a sense of my life as an adventure in time. So too, when my unfulfilled needs make themselves felt, I may come to a sense of my wholeness as a human being, a larger sense of my life encompassing not only what is present but also what is missing in my life. Indeed, seeing boundary situations and boundary conditions as meaningful, I may come to a sense that what happens is meaningful, that in some way "the right thing happens to the happy man."

What "the right thing" is, though, can look very different from the standpoint of need and from that of heart's desire. From the standpoint of need it is fulfillment. From that of heart's desire even an unfulfilled need can be meaningful. Consider Job in his affliction. Once when I was talking with a woman in Manaus about the Church of the Poor Devil, she said, "Oh yes, the Church of Poor Job." Although it is not actually called that, she was giving me the true gist of that name "the Poor Devil." If the right thing is fulfillment, then Job in his affliction is someone for whom the right thing is not happening but who has nevertheless a relationship with God. It is true, fulfillment comes to him in the end when everything

is restored to him manifold. Yet if he has a relationship with
God all along, it is because he is not reducible to his need.
Even in his outcry to God, his expression of his heart's desire,
"even in that is heaven to me." Even Job, even the Poor Devil,
even the Elephant Man can be "the happy man."

If the right things happens to me, accordingly, it will be
because I am happy, because I am turning on my own axis,
because I am orbiting around the sun. It does not happen
when I am trying to go in different directions to meet my
different needs. Then my experience becomes one of con-
straint as I feel the insistency of my needs, one of divergence
as I try to take the different directions in which they lead me,
and one of frustration as I fail ultimately to meet them. It is
the wrong thing happening to the unhappy man. When I give
expression to my heart's desire, on the other hand, when I
share with others the solitude of my own heart, my equivalent
of Job's outcry, of Cordolina's chapel, of Merrick's imitation,
the feeling of constraint gives way to one of release as I
become free to follow my own deepest longing, that of diver-
gence gives way to one of convergence as the many directions
resolve into one, and that of frustration gives way to one
of possibility as the one direction becomes an open road be-
fore me.

I conclude that the Poor Devil is happy. A paradox, I
know. I feel like Camus concluding that Sisyphus is happy,
rolling his rock up a hill. "One must imagine Sisyphus
happy."[25] One must imagine the Poor Devil happy. And yet
Sisyphus, rolling his rock up a hill, is more like a man trying
vainly to meet his needs than one following his heart's desire.
When Antonio called himself "the Poor Devil" and Cordolina
in her turn called herself "the Poor Devil," they were giving
expression to unfulfilled need. When Cordolina built her
Chapel of Santo Antonio, she was giving expression to heart's
desire. When people called her chapel "the Church of the
Poor Devil," they hit upon the paradox of heart's desire and

unfulfilled need. Somehow in that juncture of happiness and unhappiness there is the making of the soul.

The Making of the Soul

"Man makes religion," Marx says; "religion does not make man."[26] Cordolina building the Church of the Poor Devil, Le Corbusier building the Chapel at Ronchamp, Merrick making the model of Saint Phillip's are all images of the human being making religion. But if the making is a labor of love expressing a relationship with God on a human scale, as I have been saying, then it is an image also of religion making the human being, of "soul-making," as Keats named it, something that comes about in the interplay between the human heart and the circumstances of life. "I began by seeing how man was formed by circumstances," Keats says in a letter, "and what are circumstances? but touchstones of his heart? and what are touchstones? but provings of his heart? and what are provings of his heart but fortifiers or alterers of his nature? and what is his altered nature but his soul?"[27]

If I come to grips with the circumstances of my own life, with living in the solitude of my own heart, if I give expression to that solitude and to my own struggle with loneliness, I get involved in a project very similar to that of building a church, creating a space, a solitude where human beings can meet God and each other. It is like the Chapel at Ronchamp, "a project difficult, meticulous, primitive, made strong by the resources brought into play," Le Corbusier says, "but sensitive and informed by all-embracing mathematics which is the creator of that space which cannot be described in words."[28]

Soul-making too is "a project difficult, meticulous, primitive." It is difficult because it means a mastering of circumstances. I have to master my circumstances as I would master a language: learn to understand their meaning and to make of them a means of expression. It is like learning to read and to write. It would be easier simply to adjust to circumstances, "to conquer myself rather than fortune,"[29] as Descartes says, but if I try to master them, I begin to get involved in soul-searching, discovering what I am to understand and to express. Then the project becomes meticulous, a careful and conscientious and sometimes anxious examination of my deeper motives, a searching for my heart's desire. As it turns out, the understanding and the expressing are connected like the understanding and the speaking of a language. I find myself learning a language that is familiar to peoples we have called "primitive," that of the human soul and the soul of the world, where for us with our developed science and medicine the familiar language is that of the human body and the body of the world. Soul-making can be "made strong by the resources brought into play," by translating from the one language into the other. It has to be "sensitive" to new insight, though, to the new knowledge that comes from seeing body as an expression of soul, and it has to be "informed by all-embracing mathematics" when it comes to the expression of soul in bodily form. It is like reading and writing and arithmetic. There is the expression of soul in words, but there is the expression also in "that space which cannot be described in words," the human space where we live and work and play and worship.

"Now shall I make my soul," Yeats says in his poem "The Tower."[30] I say it too now as I enter into the making of the Poor Devil's soul: Now shall I make my soul! For I shall be coming into contact with what happens inside the Church of the Poor Devil, and not only inside the actual chapel but also inside the *barracão* where Zulmira showed me a lighted replica of the chapel full of saints corresponding to African gods and goddesses. The inside of the chapel is the image of an inner space and Zulmira's replica is an image of what for her and for others is truly in that space. What I shall be doing now is passing over into that space full of saints and gods and coming back to find out what is in the solitude of my own heart. If magic is a correlating of the human soul and the soul of the world, and science is a correlating of the human body and the body of the world, then religion is a correlating of soul and body.[31] That is what is happening in the Church of the Poor Devil, I believe, a correlating of soul and body. "The key is light," Le Corbusier says of the Chapel at Ronchamp, "and light illuminates shapes and shapes have an emotional power."[32] There is a kind of power in the Chapel at Ronchamp with its many odd-shaped windows and the roof set slightly above the walls on concrete columns. "Light flows down," as he says, and it is able to awaken the soul. There is power like that in the Church of the Poor Devil too, but the "shapes" that have "emotional power" here are those of the saints, those that are actually in the chapel and those in the replica that are here in imagination. What power do they have? There is the power of magic, as I am conceiving it, for the soul of the world is felt here as a manifold of gods and goddesses, and there is the power of religion, for the gods and goddesses are correlated with the human figures of the saints.

It is not that light corresponds to soul here and darkness to body. Rather the light of the soul comes into the darkness of the soul, and that is imaged, and not only imaged but actually evoked, by physical light coming into physical darkness. "The shaft of light strikes the stone in a room of utter simplicity," Dag Hammarskjold says of his Meditation Room at the United Nations. It is a room that is almost empty except for a block of iron ore and a shaft of light striking its surface. It is an image for me of the solitude of the heart. "Light flows down" here also, and here you can see how purely and simply "the key is light" and how "light illuminates shapes and shapes have an emotional power." Emptiness in the room and stillness in the soul give the power its full scope. "There are no other symbols, there is nothing to distract our attention or to break in on the stillness within ourselves," Hammarskjold says. And so there is a correlating of soul and body. "It is for those who come here," he says, "to fill the void with what they find in their center of stillness."[33]

Light plays a role in magic as well as in religion but there is not that same stillness and emptiness to lend it power. In magic the key is actually darkness, I think, the darkness of the soul, not a still and empty darkness but one that is full of the interplay of forces between the human soul (*anima hominis*) and the soul of the world (*anima mundi*), between the human heart, that is, and the larger and more impersonal forces that make themselves felt through circumstances. It is fear of the dark that frightens you away and fascination with the dark, the other side of the fear, that draws you on into the dark realm of the soul, like Childe Roland in Browning's poem "Childe Roland to the Dark Tower Came."[34] There is soul-making in coming into that realm, in coming into the interplay of forces, in coming to the Dark Tower. There can even be the building of an actual tower, like Yeats rebuilding Thoor Ballylee and Jung building Bollingen, each of them living in his tower and calling it "The Tower" and seeing it as a place of soul-making.[35] It is like and unlike Cordolina building her chapel.

When I first heard of the Church of the Poor Devil and thought it might have something to do with devil-worship, I approached it with some of the very dread and fascination that leads a person into the darkness of the soul. The same thing happened later when I heard of the Mother of the Saint and went to meet her at night. When I actually saw the Chapel of Santo Antonio, the dread and fascination passed and I came to a clear sense of the difference between magic and religion. When I actually met Zulmira too, the dread and fascination passed, but this time they passed into a kind of wonder, and I came not upon a differentiation but rather upon an integration of magic and religion,[36] where the interplay of forces that goes on in the darkness of the soul begins to come out into the light.

What is the interplay of forces? Here is where science can help, I believe. The interplay between the human soul and the soul of the world corresponds somehow to the interplay between the human body and the body of the world. What is happening in our inner experience corresponds somehow to what is happening in our outer experience. What comes to light in a tower like Bollingen or Thoor Ballylee corresponds somehow to what comes to light in a laboratory or an observatory. How? Is it a parallelism? An interaction? A single reality with an inner and an outer aspect? All the old questions about soul and body can be extended to include the soul and body of the world. The answer has to be found in correlating soul and body, and that is what is happening, I think, in places like the Meditation Room, the Chapel at Ronchamp, and the Church of the Poor Devil. It comes to light when "light flows down." The interplay of forces does not cease, it seems, even in the stillness and emptiness. It is revealed in "the play of proportions" Le Corbusier speaks of at Ronchamp, "the play of relationships unexpected, amazing," and "the intellectual play of purpose." It is transfigured. "Observe the play of shadows," he says, "learn the game. . . ."[37]

I only glimpsed the play of shadows inside the Church of the Poor Devil that first time I visited it. As my sense of the uncanny passed, nevertheless, looking inside, I was passing from the animate world of magic where every shadow is full of dread and fascination to the inanimate world of science where there are only the elements, light and shadow, walls and space, emptied of all dread and fascination ("the elements of architecture are light and shadow, walls and space")[38] to the world of religion where the elements are able to express and evoke the light and the darkness of the soul, the limits and the emptiness of the soul. Afterward when I met Zulmira, I found myself making that same transition but without passing through the inanimate world where the elements are empty of dread and fascination. Instead the shadows of the animate world, the gods and goddesses, became the human figures of the world of images.

A kind of discipline of the soul, I can see now, is needed to make good the differentiation of magic and religion, a stilling and an emptying that allows the light to flow down into the darkness of the soul. In that discipline there is an exorcising of shadows, a stilling and emptying of dread and fascination, that can leave you with nothing but the bare elements and their interplay. If you let the stillness be still, though, and the emptiness be empty, the interplay of elements can be the awakening of the soul. It is "the void," as Simone Weil calls it, and "grace" coming through the void. "The imagination is continually at work," she says, "filling up all the fissures through which grace might pass."[39] Letting the stillness be still and the emptiness be empty is letting the void be void, and the awakening of the soul is grace coming through the void. But what about the integration of magic and religion? Is turning the shadows full of dread and fascination into human figures, like the ones Zulmira showed me, the work of imagination filling the void? Or can grace come also through imagination?

There is a void that I experience whenever I am alone with myself, an inner emptiness. It is the solitude of my own heart. I am tempted always to fill it up with imaginings, with images that arise from my own hopes and fears. Letting the void be void for me, accordingly, means being willing to be in that emptiness without filling it up, being willing to live in that solitude, and waiting to see what, if anything, will arise out of the stillness when my usual hopes and fears are in suspense. Grace coming through the void then is the presence I begin to feel when all is still and empty. There is the presence of God. Yet there are human presences there too, human figures. They are the other persons I meet there as I find all human hearts dwelling in the same solitude. It is a "communion of saints," like the fellowship of all Christ's followers living and dead, a connection that is based on the presence of God in the solitude of every heart.

Imagination is not annihilated, therefore, though it is changed, in letting the void be void. It is imagination that is sensitive to the presence of God and to human presences in the solitude of the heart, like film that is sensitive to light. I can envision three stages here, corresponding in slow motion to the three stages I passed through so quickly in looking inside the Church of the Poor Devil. First there is a stage where imagination is shaped very largely by a person's circumstances and conditioning, where it is difficult to imagine things being other than they have been, where the power of imagination is felt mostly in the form of dread and fascination, the unknown investing the known world. Then comes a stage where imagination is being purified of dread and fascination, where it is becoming possible to imagine all kinds of permutations and combinations of the elements of the known world, where imagination is beginning to range through an infinity of possible worlds. Finally there comes a stage where the elements of the world become images to imagination, where time becomes "a changing image of eternity,"[40] where light becomes an image of the light and shadow of the darkness, walls of the limits and space of the emptiness of the soul. It is then that the soul awakens.

Grace comes through the void, by stilling imagination and emptying it of dread and fascination. That is what I find in the solitude of my own heart. Grace also comes through imagination, by giving human shape to the powers of life and death. That is what I find in the array of saints corresponding to gods and goddesses that fill the replica of the Church of the Poor Devil. Imagination is being redeemed here when otherwise it would become an outer darkness. It makes a difference, though, if I go through the moment of differentiation before I come to that of integration, if I enter the desolation, the still and empty void, where I find God and my own humanity. For then I come to a "communion of saints" who are all equally human beings and who all share a relationship with God. I become free of the powers of life and death.

My imagination is never free so long as I am haunted by the shadows of dread and fascination. A slave, according to Hegel, is one who lives in "the fear of death, the sovereign master."[41] There is a freedom and a slavery of the imagination—not an imaginary freedom and slavery, to be sure, but a slavery that takes hold of a person through imagination and the fear of death and a freedom that comes about through an awakening of soul when you awaken from dread as from a nightmare and from fascination as from a dream. As long as I am under the spell of the dream and the nightmare it is as if I were obsessed or even possessed by some power greater than myself, by some god or goddess. As soon as the spell is broken, on the other hand, although I am still able to feel the fear and the lure, it is as if I had become free of the gods and had returned to myself. Hegel speaks of "death, the sovereign master," but all the gods and goddesses can be experienced in this fashion, not only death but all the powers of the universe, those of life and those of death. Yet it is death where the power of dread is greatest.

According to Hegel, freedom will come to me through work, for I am able to say, "I am" through my work and that is an answer to "I will die."[42] That seems true when I think of Cordolina building the Church of the Poor Devil or Le Corbusier building the Chapel at Ronchamp or Merrick making the model of Saint Phillip's. The idea seems untrue, however, when I think of actual laborers and their work unless they are "free and masters of their craft," as Le Corbusier says of his workers. Otherwise their work says only, "I will die." I think of the sign Elie Wiesel saw at Auschwitz, "Work is liberty."[43] It was a travesty of Hegel's idea, no doubt, but it can serve as a warning, for its contrast with the reality of life in a death camp, to differentiate between work that is freeing and work that is enslaving.

Imagination begins to be free, it seems, only when something more powerful than the fear of death is awakened, something that can cast out "the fear of death, the sovereign master," like the love that "casts out fear."[44] Say I have been living in an image of life that has been shaped primarily by death. I relate to death as if it really were "the sovereign master"; I live in the fear of death; I wait on death. Actually I saw not long ago on a clock face the inscription "Night cometh," and it evoked all this imagery in me. I thought of my age and how little time I have left. Afterward I realized the words are from the Gospel of John and in their context they evoke a rather different image of life. "I must work the works of him that sent me, while it is day," Jesus says there: "The night cometh, when no man can work."[45] God does not correspond to death in those words. Jesus does what God is doing while the day of life lasts; the night of death comes when no one can do anything. It is one thing, therefore, to relate to God and another thing to relate to death as "the sovereign master." It is the difference between God and the gods.

Say I begin to live in this new image of life. It is an image of doing what God is doing while it is day, like sunflower heads turning with the sun from dawn to twilight. I can see Le Corbusier working with an image of what God is doing when he says, "Light flows down," and Merrick when he speaks of "grace flying up and up from the mud," and Hammarskjold when he says, "The shaft of light strikes the stone in a room of utter simplicity." It is still true, "Night cometh." Hammarskjold begins the later entries in his diary each year with the words "Night is drawing nigh," but he comes at last to an insight. "Do not seek death," he tells himself. "Death will find you. But seek the road which makes death a fulfillment."[46]

Imagination is truly free, I conclude, when it can imagine "the road which makes death a fulfillment." Soul awakens on that road and time and the elements become images to imagination. It is the road that opens up before me when I am letting the void be void and grace is coming through the void. The ultimate void is death. If I can expect grace to come through that void, the presence of God and human presences as in the solitude of my own heart, then I am on a road that makes even death a fulfillment. The paradox of the road is that fullness comes through emptiness. It is not that life and death simply lose their dread and fascination for me and become devoid of wonder. Stilling imagination and emptying it of dread and fascination has the effect rather of making it like the world in the beginning, when "the earth was without form and void, and darkness was upon the face of the deep; and the Spirit of God was moving over the face of the water."[47]

According to Kierkegaard, dread can be "a saving experience by means of faith." The same is true of fascination, I think, the other side of dread, even the dread and fascination that plunge you into the darkness of the soul. You sink into the abyss of dread and fascination but then you float up from the depth, "lighter now than all that is oppressive and dreadful in life."[48] The saving experience occurs at the bottom where dread is no longer dreadful and fascination is no longer fascinating, where "the soul begins to tremble into stillness."[49] It occurs in the void of imagination, that is, when you are letting the void be void and grace is coming through the void. For there in the void you discover the place where all dread and fascination arise, where all images arise and all religion, where the world itself is created.

The Religion of the Poor

Is Christianity a Church of the Poor Devil? That is the question that occurs to me now as I reflect upon Christianity and its power to awaken a heart's desire that is more powerful than the fear of death. Simone Weil, recalling how she saw women singing in a procession in a Portuguese fishing village, says, "There the conviction was suddenly borne in upon me that Christianity is preeminently the religion of slaves, that slaves cannot help belonging to it, and I among others."[50] That is what I am seeing too—with this difference, that an awakening of the soul can mean not only realizing you are a slave but also becoming free. In Peru, for example, there is a cult of the Purple Christ (*Cristo Morado*), the Lord of the Maltreated (*Señor de los maltratados*), originally an African slave religion, where the poor and oppressed are assimilated to Christ in his sufferings. It is at once an expression of suffering and "a symbolic resistance"[51] to enslavement. There are ways of casting out the fear of death that are themselves deadly, it is true, murderous and suicidal, like the mass suicide that occurred at Jonestown in Guyana among the members of the People's Temple. That too was a religion of the poor. Is it possible to cast out the fear of death without falling into the power of "death, the sovereign master"?

I see an answer here in the connection between popular and personal religion. "Inside, alone with yourself," Le Corbusier says of the Chapel at Ronchamp. "Outside, ten thousand pilgrims in front of the altar."[52] Inside, personal religion, he is saying; outside, popular religion. To be sure, I cannot say, "Inside, alone with yourself" of the Church of the Poor Devil. "Inside, many images of saints who are also gods and goddesses" would be more like it, thinking of what Zulmira showed me, and "outside, many people gathered for the procession of Santo Antonio," thinking of what I saw there during the festival in June. Popular religion, that is, both inside and outside. Still, there is a continuity between that inner space full of images and the void of imagination in the solitude of the heart, and there is a continuity also between the procession of people with lighted candles, an image of the journey together, and the personal journey in time.

That continuity can be my way into the religion of the poor. When Simone Weil speaks of Christianity as "the religion of slaves" and says, "Slaves cannot help belonging to it, and I among others," she is crossing over to popular religion from personal religion. It is like Katherine Anne Porter speaking of the "ship of fools" and saying, "I am a passenger on that ship," crossing over to the journey together from the personal journey. Simone Weil's formula, "and I among others," carries with it the personal certainties, "I am" and "I will die," and especially "I will die." Somehow the one certainty, "I am," seems to set personal life apart. For it is an affirmation, even an assertion, of personal existence. The other certainty, "I will die," seems to draw a person into the journey together and the religion of the poor. For it can be a confession of personal morality, almost like "Pray for us sinners, now and at the hour of our death."[53] If I start, as I actually do, with a sense of my life as an adventure and God as my companion, I can find my way into the journey together and the religion of the poor as I realize that the adventure is in time and that the hour of my death approaches.

Once I am there, sharing in the journey together and in the religion of the poor, I have to come to terms with death and find my way back into life. I see a danger there in the dread and fascination of death. It is the danger of a willing subjection to "death, the sovereign master." "There I received forever the mark of a slave," Simone Weil says of the time she spent working in a factory. "Since then I have always regarded myself as a slave."[54] Finding my way back into life, I can see, will mean finding my way into freedom. It will mean seeing how God, having no limiting essence, is unlike death, is no limit on human existence. Let me try to pass over into the religion of the poor, therefore, going over by way of death and coming back by way of life.

It is the experience of "perpetual light"[55] that speaks to the certainty "I will die," an experience I saw imaged in the candles left burning outside the Church of the Poor Devil at night, "lighted candles, *promessas*, that signify hours of affliction, moments of hope."[56] A friend once told me he saw his own spirit in that image of a candle burning—he wished he could blow out the candle, he said, but knew he could not. I was surprised that death was not the problem for him but immortality. He was not afraid the candle would go out, that he would die. At least he was not thinking of that at the time. Rather he felt the burden of immortality, the inability to blow out the candle. I thought of Kierkegaard speaking of "the eternal in man" and saying, "But the eternal he cannot get rid of, no, not to all eternity."[57] There is a desire to die, I could see, as well as a desire to live. Somehow the two go together in the heart's desire, the desire to die appearing in "hours of affliction," and the desire to live in "moments of hope." A life that is full of affliction, a life of poverty and deprivation, can be full of a desire to die. So it appears in "hours of affliction." Yet it can be full also of a desire to live. And so it appears in "moments of hope."

What is "perpetual light"? It is an experience, I believe, where the desire to die meets the desire to live. It is a manifestation of "eternal life," the deeper life that is spoken of in the Gospel of John. That deeper life is a turning on the axis of human existence while orbiting around the sun that is God's existence, the heart's desire, I think, both as desire to live and as desire to die. At the heart of murder there is suicide, I was saying when speaking of "the heart of light and of darkness,"[58] but at the heart of suicide there is rebirth, I must say now, a desire for a new life. The desire to die can become suicidal and murderous, as at Jonestown, but when it is integrated with the desire to live it becomes the heart's desire for a deeper life, a life that is hidden in "hours of affliction" and revealed in "moments of hope." When the integration occurs, when the desire to die meets the desire to live, then light is kindled, the candle is lit, a perpetual light shines in the darkness of the soul.

If I enter into the experience of "hours of affliction," I come upon the desire to die in its naked form. "A heart-rending sadness" is what Simone Weil heard in the songs of the fishing village, and in the factory, she says, "The affliction of others entered into my flesh and my soul."[59] The word she is using here and elsewhere for "affliction" is *malheur*, "misery" or "unhappiness." It is one thing to go through your own times of unhappiness; it is another to let the misery of others enter, as she does, into your flesh and your soul. When you are going through your own times of trouble, your unhappiness seems to cling to your own personal existence and it seems that death would be an escape from personal existence and thus also an escape from misery. When you let the distress of others enter into your flesh and your soul, as she does, then it can seem that personal existence itself is an escape from pain and affliction, an escape somehow from the common lot of human beings, and the acceptance of death can seem more like an acceptance of the common suffering, a willingness to belong to the human race. So the desire to die can change, as it does for her, from a wish to escape from suffering to a willingness to undergo suffering.

Say I do accept my own death with this thought in mind, that in saying, "I will die" I am saying Yes to belonging to the human race, to being a passenger on the "ship of fools," even to being one among others in "the religion of slaves." A change comes over me as I do this, a change in the very prototype of my life. I had been living without knowing it, let us say, according to the prototype that Yeats calls the "forerunner" and the "successor" of Christ, one who mourns "over the shortness of time, and man's inadequacy to his fate." Now I am beginning to live according to the prototype of Christ himself, one who "mourns over the length of years," Yeats says, "and the inadequacy of man's fate to man."[60]

When I was living my own life and going my own journey, I

was feeling "the shortness of time," the shortness, that is, of my own life and the shortness generally of human life. It seemed I would have to die before I had fulfilled my desire to live. Now, as I plunge myself into the journey together, I am beginning to feel "the length of years," not the length of my own years or of my life but that of "dark times" of war and famine and sickness and death, times when death rather than God seems to reign over human affairs. I am beginning now to wait on God instead of death. When I was feeling the shortness of time, I was feeling also "the inadequacy of man to his fate," and especially my own inadequacy to my own fate, wasting my life, not making full use of the short time I did have. If I could only embrace my own personal existence and be willing to walk alone, I thought, all the things I lacked would come to me. Now, as I do begin to walk in that willingness, I find myself on a journey with everyone else and I am starting to feel rather "the inadequacy of man's fate to man," not the inadequacy of my own personal fate so much as that of the common fate. My willingness to be in need places me with those who are in need.

Yet there is a critique of Christianity implied in Yeats's words about Christ. "One that feels but for the common lot," he says, describing Christ, "and mourns over the length of years and the inadequacy of man's fate to man." There is the implication that "one that feels but for the common lot" lacks a feeling for personal destiny. "Two thousand years before," he says, "his predecessor, careful of heroic men alone, had so stood and mourned over the shortness of time, and man's inadequacy to his fate."[61] He is thinking here of a figure like Oedipus who goes from disagreement to agreement with his personal destiny, who in spite of his terrible fate ends by saying "all is well."[62] And Yeats imagines there will be a successor now two thousand years after Christ who will see things in a way very similar to that of Oedipus, someone like Nietzsche's Zarathustra who says, "Yes and Amen"[63] to all the joys and sorrows of life, willing to live them over and over in an eternal recurrence.

An answer to the critique comes to light if I enter into the experience of "moments of hope." There I see the desire to die turning over into the desire to live and an assurance developing in the midst of affliction like that of Juliana of Norwich, "All will be well, and all will be well, and every kind of thing will be well."[64] It corresponds in some ways to Oedipus saying, "All is well," and to Zarathustra saying, "Yes and Amen," but there is a difference. The contrast appears in the two sentences, "All is well" and "All will be well." If I say, "All is well," like Oedipus at Colonus or like Zarathustra willing the eternal recurrence of all events, I am consenting to my situation, to my circumstances, to the human condition itself, I am turning my lot and the common lot insofar as I share it into a personal destiny. There is something of that in the religion of the poor too whenever people say, "It is the will of God," but that is said with sorrow. If I say, "All will be well," like Juliana, I am not simply accepting my lot and the common lot, I am looking to the events of life for a meaning, I am hoping affliction will lead into joy.

Is hope then a feeling for personal destiny? If I start from a feeling for "the shortness of time," hope can seem an illusion, as it did to Nietzsche, and personal destiny a beauty in life that appears only when the illusion of hope is taken away. So too if I start from a feeling for "the length of years," personal hope can seem an illusion, as it did to Marx, and human destiny a communal hope that appears only when the illusion of personal hope is destroyed. If I pass over into "moments of hope," however, I enter into a relationship with God where time is relative, where the shortness and the length of time seem to be the illusion rather than hope, where I can see the connection between my own lot and the common lot, between hope for me and hope for everyone.

It is in the passage through "hours of affliction" to

"moments of hope" that I find here a feeling for human destiny. If I go through affliction to hope with the poor, I find myself reenacting with them the story of Jesus, going through death to resurrection. It is like joining the procession of the women singing in the Portuguese fishing village or that of the *maltratados* in Lima honoring El Cristo Morado or that of the people at the Church of the Poor Devil, a procession I actually did join, carrying lighted candles in honor of Santo Antonio. "The cross—the true cross of suffering—is raised up in this space," Le Corbusier says of the great cross at Ronchamp; "the drama of Christianity has taken possession of the place from this time onwards."[65] There is no great cross like that in the Church of the Poor Devil, only the white cross on top and the crucifix inside on the altar. There is a feeling for "the drama of Christianity," nevertheless, in the candles carried in the procession and left burning on the threshold at night. "The light shines in the darkness," as in the Gospel of John, "and the darkness has not overcome it."[66] There is a darkness and thus there is affliction, but a light shines in the darkness and thus there is hope. What is the darkness? What is the hope?

"Sin is necessary" ("sin is behovely"), Juliana says, and that is the darkness, "but all will be well, and all will be well, and every kind of thing will be well," and that is the hope. Under "sin is necessary" you can include both "man's inadequacy to his fate" and "the inadequacy of man's fate to man." The one is linked with the other in her thinking and in popular religion ("it is true that sin is the cause of all this pain").[67] Under "all will be well" you can include both a personal and a communal hope. There too the one is linked with the other, for the hope is centered on one figure, that of Christ, who is an individual and yet is prototype of many. The women in the fishing village, the *maltratados*, the people at the Church of the Poor Devil, are all assimilated to that figure, are all of them "poor devils" who go through affliction to joy.

Here again a critique of Christianity can be drawn up from the standpoint of personal destiny. "Christ is an exemplar who dwells in every Christian as his integral personality," Jung says. "But historical trends led to the *imitatio Christi*, whereby the individual does not pursue his own destined road to wholeness, but attempts to imitate the way taken by Christ."[68] If I try to pass over from personal religion to the religion of the poor, as I am doing, I become especially liable to this critique. For I seem to be abandoning my own "destined road to wholeness" and trying to walk the road of the poor, the hungry, the sorrowful, the outcast, "the way taken by Christ." My own way is to follow my own lights, to take the insights that come to me, one by one, as gifts, as enlightenment and guidance and assurance, leading me to become who I am meant to be. If I try to follow Christ, then I am taking Christ for my light, seeking the insights that come from following him through affliction to joy, relying on them, on him, for comfort and counsel, and becoming all the while, as I follow his path through affliction, a "poor devil" myself.

An answer can be found in the actual experience of going through affliction to hope. For it is in such an experience, when it takes the form of an encounter with death, that you actually discover the road of your personal destiny. Here is the song we sang every night at the Church of the Poor Devil during the novena and on the night of the festival during the procession:

Cheios de fé e confiança,	Full of faith and confidence,
De ti rogamos proteção;	We ask of you protection;
Vem nos dar perseverança	Come give us perseverance
Que nos valha de eternal	That may avail us of eternal
visão.	vision.[69]

It speaks of hope and "eternal vision," the vision of God, that is, at death. If you see God leading you there step by step, "eternal vision" becomes a personal destiny. I think of Newman coming near death as a young man when he was ill in Sicily and then on his voyage home writing the lines "Lead, Kindly Light." He has to follow insights one by one in follow-ing the "kindly light" of Christ:

> I do not ask to see
> The distant scene; one step enough for me.[70]

Light is the same in personal religion, I believe, as in the religion of the poor; "the way taken by Christ" and the road of personal destiny are one and the same. If there is a difference, it is in the following of insights one by one. "Man awaits death and judgment with nothing to occupy the worldly faculties," Yeats says, criticizing the historic effect of Christianity, "and helpless before the world's disorder, drags out of the subconscious the conviction that the world is about to end."[71] Without the sense of being led step by step, the time between now and the ultimate fulfillment of hope drops away into insignificance, and it can seem there is "nothing to occupy the worldly faculties" or else "the world is about to end," and waiting on God is still not fully differentiated from waiting on death. But if I have the sense of following insights one by one, then the time immediately ahead becomes significant, "I do not ask to see the distant scene," and I become occupied with taking the next step, "one step enough for me." And if that sense of following insights becomes a common sense, a high-way rather than a private way, then waiting on death can give way to waiting on God, and "the religion of slaves" can become the religion of the free.

What happens in personal religion, I am thinking, can happen also in the religion of the poor. A movement toward freedom does in fact occur in "the religions of the oppressed,"[72] as they have been called, such as the Native American Church among the Indians of North America and the many native churches of Africa. What I have in mind, though, is something based on the inner exigencies of Christianity itself rather than on the opposition of one culture to another. When I think of the Church of the Poor Devil, I am thinking of something much smaller than a native church, a tiny chapel, and the people who light candles there and come there for the festival, and yet of something much larger too, Christianity as religion of the poor.

It is the awakening of soul, if anything, that can overcome the sense of being "helpless before the world's disorder" and open the way to freedom. There is an awakening of soul, I find, in passing over from personal religion to the religion of the poor, entering into "hours of affliction" and "moments of hope." I go from concern about personal destiny to concern about the common fate, from feelings surrounding my relation to the things of life to feelings surrounding the things themselves, the common joys and sorrows.[73] Coming into these feelings with a strong sense of personal existence, I end up not simply sharing the common joys and sorrows but entering into a conscious relationship with them, feeling the inadequacy of the common fate. Maybe there is a reciprocal awakening for a person who starts from the religion of the poor and passes over to personal religion, coming from an immersion in the things of life and the common joys and sorrows to a sense of having a relationship with things and thus a personal existence. Here too there can be a coming back again to the original and strongest feelings, those surrounding the things of life, but there can be a new awareness as well, acquired from passing over, a sense of entering into a conscious relationship with things one by one.

Insight by insight I discover my way on my personal journey in life. Something similar can happen on the journey together, I think, and when it does we lose the sense of being "helpless before the world's disorder." I have a relationship with my lot in life, and that is the basis of my personal journey, but my lot also has a relationship with me, and that is the basis of my participation in our journey together. When I go through affliction, my relation with my lot changes, as I come by suffering to new insight, but I am looking for a change also in its relation with me, from its being a sorrow to being a joy. If I go with the poor through affliction, I come to many insights that arise out of sorrow, like Simone Weil's realization, "the religion of slaves" and "I among others." Yet as insights they enlighten rather than darken the heart. By following them I seem to be walking with the poor on a road that is leading into joy.

One insight is that into heart's desire, seeing and understanding what it is that people actually want, especially what poor people want. Rilke has a story called "Why God Wants Poor People."[74] God wants to see what human beings are like, he says, when they are stripped down to their bare humanity. If I were to write a converse story called "Why Poor People Want God," it would have to be a story of heart's desire. Poor people want God not because they are poor, I would have to say, not because they are naked human beings but because they are human beings. If human beings are like the earth, the simile I have been using, they want God as the earth wants the sun. The earth does not plunge into the sun, but it orbits around the sun while turning on its own axis. Poor people, and people generally, if I am right, want to orbit around God, have a relationship with God, while turning on their own axis, living a human existence. God then is not simply an escape from a human existence that has been stripped of everything that makes it desirable. Rather God makes existence desirable even when people have been stripped to their bare humanity. It is true, as Rilke implies, that riches conceal that bare humanity and poverty reveals it. So also poverty reveals the desire for God. It reveals the desire to die too, the desire to escape from an existence that is pervaded by affliction.

Another insight then is to differentiate waiting on God from waiting on death. When they are undifferentiated, death can seem like God and God like death. Just as death takes everything away and strips human beings to their bare humanity, revealing them naked in their utter mortality, so it can seem that "God wants poor people," and all the feelings surrounding death can surround God, the dread and the fascination, the sorrow expressed in elegy, the lamentation of death and of unrequited love. Yet there is a discipline of soul that can go with bare humanity, a stilling and an emptying of soul, as we have seen, that allows light to flow down into the soul. There is a making of soul, an inner coming to life, that links God with life rather than death. Still, the role death plays in the making of soul points to an integration of death into life.

A third insight, accordingly, is to integrate the desire to die and the desire to live. Speaking out of the desire to die, as it seems, Rilke says God is "the final fruit of a tree whose leaves we are."[75] God is the last thing of all, he is saying, just as death is the last thing of life. If I speak out of the desire to live, I have to say God is the first thing of all, the source of life, but if I conjoin the desire to die and the desire to live, then I have to say God is in death as well as in life, *God is the heart's desire*. If I see God only in death, I will say, as Rilke does, "God wants poor people," God is at work in time, that is, reducing human beings to their bare humanity. But if I see God in life as well as in death, I will say, as I have in effect, "poor people want God," that is, God is leading human beings by the heart. And if I meditate on something like the Church of the Poor Devil, where I can see the religion of the poor, I am led to answer my own question, "Why do poor people want God?" out of a vision of the road on which we travel when we follow the heart's desire.

On that road I am with the Poor Devil, the Saint, the Mother of the Saint, the people who light candles at night, the people who come for the festival, I am walking with them on Christ's way through affliction to joy. It is like the earth following the sun's way, revolving around the sun as the sun moves through the galaxy. There is the night by night rhythm of the people lighting candles, expressing the hopes and afflictions of a human existence, like the earth turning on its axis, and there is the year by year rhythm of the people coming to the festival, expressing the course of their life in relation with God, like the earth orbiting around the sun, but there is also the road of the journey, and the sense of being led insight by insight, like the sun's way through the darkness of the universe.

THREE

The Way of
Heart's Desire

On the night of the festival people gathered around the Church of the Poor Devil, nearly a thousand of them, it seemed to me, most of them poor people, though there were a few also from the upper class. They looked at me, wondering who I was and where I came from, until an old black woman, she must have been a hundred years old, came up and began to speak with me. We had spoken also on the previous nights at the novena and in the morning at the blessing of the bread. Then there had been fewer people, more like fifty. Now, as the others saw us talking, they smiled and looked away and I became one of them. Candles were passed around after a while, and we lit them and relit each other's again and again whenever they were blown out in the evening breeze. We walked in procession, without any particular order, in the middle of streets, from the Church of the Poor Devil to the larger Church of Santa Rita a few blocks away. When we entered the large and lighted space of the church, we sang our song of "eternal vision" (*eternal visão*).¹ It all seemed an image somehow of life's journey, walking together in the dark, carrying our candles, and coming at last into a place of light. A way seemed to open up before us, a way leading through the darkness of life to an eternal vision. And yet life was not all darkness. There was the light of the candles we were carrying and there was the sharing of light with one another as we relit one another's candles every time they were blown out in the wind. That is the essence of a way, that there be some mode of gaining life and some mode of sharing it with one another. Also there is the connection between the light along the way and the place of light into which we came, between the way and the goal. If my way is that of gaining insight and sharing insight with others, then the gaining of insight is my way of relating with God (as in the prayer "Lead, Kindly Light"), while the sharing of insight is my way of relating with others.

"Eternal vision" is the goal. Each insight along the way, if I am living toward such a goal, seems a distant glow of that final illumination breaking upon the horizon of my mind. It is something, though, to realize your deepest longing is to see God. Usually the longing takes many different forms, one after another, as you go from enthusiasm to enthusiasm, before you realize it has anything to do with God or with a vision that is eternal. Living to see God is a way, a personal way because it means coming to personal knowledge but a common way when you realize you are doing it, as in our song of "eternal vision," because it means sharing whatever awareness you have with others, as in our lighting and relighting one another's candles as we walked together in the streets. It means seeing how lives converge. I had come to the festival with my own way, "the particular way,"² as Martin Buber calls it, the way of the personal journey, but I found there a "larger way, where many paths and errands meet," as if to say "there was only one Road; that it was like a great river: its springs were at every doorstep, and every path was its tributary."³

It is this "larger way" I want to travel now in thought. Coming to it from a personal way of gaining and sharing insight, I see it as a way of gaining and sharing life, a life that is light as in the Gospel of John, "In him was life, and the life was the light of men."[4] It is a way of living clear down in your heart. Under the sign of human needs, I can imagine, people are able to live together in a classless society, giving according to their ability and receiving according to their needs. It is a goal never yet attained. But Marx's formula, "From each according to his ability, to each according to his needs,"[5] can also be used to describe a way. Under the sign of heart's desire, I wonder, are we able to live together even now, giving according to our ability and receiving according to our needs?

The Poor Devil's Way

As we walked in the dark streets in our procession from the Church of the Poor Devil, our candles were not the only light. There were bonfires along the way and fireworks. "There is music and songs," an old account of the festival reads, "fireworks and joy."[6] I felt the joy in the procession, and I wondered at it, thinking of the poverty in which these people live, thinking of how few of them live into old age and how many die of the diseases of poverty, diarrhea and dysentery, malaria and tuberculosis. "How beautiful St. Peter's Day is," a black woman wrote in her diary while she was living in a slum of São Paulo. "Why is it that the saints of June are honored with fire?"[7] Her diary, *Child of the Dark*, is a story of almost unrelieved darkness, telling of what it is to be poor, to be hungry, to be unhappy, to be outcast. If I read it in the light of the beatitudes in the Gospel of Luke, "Blessed are you poor, . . . you that hunger now, . . . you that weep now, . . . you when men hate you,[8] . . . I find myself looking for light in the darkness. I look for a way out of misery to blessedness or for a blessedness in misery or for a way through misery to blessedness.

A friend who was homeless once wrote to me, saying, "I am not happy. I feel both joy and sadness." That is what I find also in the diary of the woman who was poor. She is not happy, but she feels both joy and sadness. Not being happy went for my friend with being homeless; it goes for the woman who was poor with living in the slum, so much so that her whole object becomes to escape, as she does in the end. Joy and sadness go not so much with homelessness or with living in a slum, not so much with the conditions of life as with life itself, with the actual events of life. All three, unhappiness and joy and sadness, are interrelated with one another, but they seem to point in different ways if I look to them for a direction. *Which is the way?* Not being happy points toward finding a home or escaping from the slum; joy points toward the inner richness of life; sadness points toward the wisdom that comes from suffering.

"Drop, drop—in our sleep, upon the heart sorrow falls, memory's pain," Aeschylus says, "and to us, though against our very will, even in our own despite, comes wisdom by the awful grace of God."[9] There is an interrelation among unhappiness and joy and sadness. It is the connection of lack and letting go and loss. In lack there is unhappiness; in letting go there is joy; in loss there is sadness. "Memory's pain" is that of loss, but it has an affinity with the unhappiness that comes from lack and also with the joy that comes from letting go. That affinity is perceived in the "wisdom" that comes "by the awful grace of God." That perceiving, that wisdom, I expect, is already the beginning of the "eternal vision" we sang about in the Church of the Poor Devil. It is a knowing of heart's desire that is already a beginning of heart's realization. To act on that wisdom, I expect also, is already to give according to our ability and to receive according to our needs. For such giving and receiving is a relating to the things of life that comes of being heart-free and heart-whole.

If there is a way of heart's desire, accordingly, it will be the way of wisdom that comes "by the awful grace of God," not just the wisdom itself, to be sure, but the way that opens up when we are acting upon the wisdom. I will suppose knowing rather than unknowing, therefore, remembering rather than forgetting in the lives of the poor. Let me try to pass over into those lives, looking for light in the darkness, looking for "the awful grace of God" that can work "even in our own despite" and "against our very will," changing our despair into hope and our will into willingness to act.

Looking for light in the darkness, I find only darkness unless I bring eyes that can see light there, eyes of faith, I mean, like the eyes with which Rouault sees human misery in his *Miserere*. In that series of engravings Rouault combines and alternates images of the suffering Christ with those of suffering humanity. Without the images of Christ those of humanity can seem, as they truly are, images of anguish and abandonment and despair. Seeing them side by side with those of Christ, the image called "the condemned is led away" and that of Christ "forever scourged"[10] for instance where the two figures, the condemned and Christ, are in exactly the same posture, stripped to the waist, head bowed and arms down, you can see something in the images of suffering humanity that is really there but that you would not otherwise see, something that casts a light on the face of anguish and abandonment and despair. I think of the faces I saw in our procession that night from the Church of the Poor Devil. The candles we were carrying illumined our faces. I could not see my own face but I could see the faces of the others, faces of suffering, some of them, and yet illumined by the candlelight.

We could not see our own faces illumined but only those of others. "But how can we forgo being recognized, at least by those nearest to us, in the reality that we ourselves do not know, but at best can only live?"[11] Our faces illumined seemed to suggest "being recognized," but not seeing our own faces seemed to suggest "the reality that we ourselves do not know." There is indeed a reality we live and do not know, I think, and it is that of the heart's desire. We can see it sometimes, not directly but in the eyes of others, when they are responding to something in us deeper than what we are trying to show them. To go through suffering, through lack and letting go and loss, is to "live" that reality, to experience the unfulfillment of the heart's desire. To come to wisdom, however, is to come to know the heart. Seeing one another's faces illumined, we can lead one another to wisdom, but not seeing our own faces, we cannot lead ourselves.

"Sometimes the blind has comforted the one who sees,"[12] Rouault writes under one of his engravings where a blind man is shown leading a man who can see. That is what happens, it seems, in coming to wisdom. I am blind because I cannot see my own face, but if my face is illumined I can comfort another person who can see it. So too another can comfort me. If I take this as my method, it leads me directly to the heart of deprivation. A blind man can be the image of wisdom here, a blind man who can see with the heart. A moment of light occurs in the darkness of that diary, *Child of the Dark*, when the woman who is poor meets a man who is blind:

I met a blind man.
"How many years ago did you lose your sight?"
"Ten years."
"Did you find it terrible?"
"No, because everything God does is good."
"What was the reason you went blind?"
"Weakness."
"There was no possibility to cure them?"
"No. Only if they were transplanted. But I needed to find someone who would give me his eyes."
"Then you have seen the sun, the flowers, and the sky filled with stars?"
"I've seen them. Thanks to God."[13]

The blind man's face is illumined, and he comforts the woman who is poor. Or so I suppose, for she records his words without comment. And yet her own face is illumined too, I realize now as I think on it, not because of his words but because of her own words in her diary, because she is truthful to the darkness of her life, because she tells what it is to be poor, to be hungry, to be unhappy, to be outcast.

If I pass over to the blind man, I find light in the darkness as I had originally hoped. He is able to say, like Hammarskjold at the turning point in his diary, "For all that has been—Thanks! To all that shall be—Yes!"[14] He is able to say that in spite of his blindness, as Hammarskjold is able to say it in spite of his loneliness. I am able to enter into that, putting my own loneliness where his blindness is. What is more, he is able to say his "Thanks!" and his "Yes!" without regret. So it is not simply resignation. Rather there is a letting go that transfigures loss and lack, a joy that is deeper than sadness and unhappiness. His "Thanks!" is for having "seen the sun, the flowers, and the sky filled with stars," and his "Yes!" is to being blind himself rather than having someone else "give me his eyes."

If I pass over to the woman who was poor, I find almost unrelieved darkness, as it seems, until I realize that her truthfulness to the darkness of her life is itself light. There is joy, it is true, in the midst of the sadness and unhappiness. "I am very happy. I sing every morning," she writes early on in her diary. "I'm like the birds who sing only in the morning because in the morning I'm always happy. The first thing that I do is open the window and think about heaven." Mostly, though, her life is misery. "How horrible it is to see a child eat and ask: 'Is there more?' " she writes further on. "This word 'more' keeps ringing in the mother's head as she looks in the pot and doesn't have any more." She sees the enormity of it all when she sees a face that is not illumined by any joy or hope, that of a woman who has just arrived in the slum (the *favela*). "She looked at the favela with its mud and sickly children. It was the saddest look I'd ever seen. Perhaps she has no more illusions. She had given her life over to misery." Her own face is like that too, and if it is illumined, it is because of her truthfulness to that misery. "There will be those who reading what I write will say—this is untrue. But misery is real."[15] Passing over to her for me means acknowledging that the light I was looking for in her darkness is not to be found. There is another light, that of truthfulness, and that is wisdom too, and you can also act upon it.

There is hope, as it turns out, even in the light of this truthfulness to misery. It appears if I set the two images side by side, the blind man and the woman who was poor, as Rouault sets the images of Christ side by side with those of suffering humanity. I see a horizon then in the horizonless prospect of misery. It is like setting the Gospels side by side with the Book of Job. What emerges from the Book of Job too is a truthfulness to misery, but something else emerges as well, as happened for me in passing over to the woman who was poor, a regard for that truthfulness as wisdom—the Book of Job is one of the Wisdom Books. When you set the figure of Job side by side with that of Christ then, that wisdom becomes a "light" that "shines in the darkness."[16] A hope appears where there seemed to be no grounds for hope, a "hope against hope,"[17] and with the prospect of hope a way of acting upon truthfulness to misery.

I see a horizon when I see, as the blind man does, with a heart that can see "the light" that "shines in the darkness." He is like the blind man in the Gospel of John. When he is asked, "Did you find it terrible?" to go blind and he answers, "No, because everything God does is good," he is pointing not simply to an acceptance of misery as the will of God, I am supposing, but to a meaning that is hidden in his misery, a meaning that is revealed when he comes face to face with "the light"—"It was not that this man sinned, or his parents, but that the works of God might be made manifest in him."[18] There is a correspondence between the blind man's phrase "everything God does" and Jesus' phrase "the works of God."

The "why" of blindness is like the "why" of loneliness. "Did'st Thou give me this inescapable loneliness," Hammarskjold writes in his diary, "so that it would be easier for me to give Thee all?"[19] The blind man in the Gospel of John comes to see with his eyes, it is true, when he comes to see with his heart. The blind man in the woman's diary comes only to see with his heart. Still, he enters by that into an "eternal vision" that begins now during his life time. It is indeed like seeing a horizon, an edge of sight.

A horizonless grind, on the other hand, is all that appears at first in the woman's diary apart from her meeting with the blind man and her moments of joy. Every day begins as the diary ends, "I got up at five and went to get water." The only horizon she sees is the prospect of escaping from the *favela*, and that proves ultimately to be a false horizon. For though she does escape for a time from the "garbage dump" as she calls it and does come to live in a "brick house" as she had dreamed, she is forced by circumstances after some years to return to live in a *favela* and to die in poverty. She is disillusioned, more unhappy than before she escaped. "One can live better when one is poor than when one is rich," she concludes. "Perhaps that is why Jesus Christ chose to be poor."[20] That could mean simply giving up and acquiescing in poverty. Or it could mean something more hopeful, living out of a truthfulness to the condition of people who are poor. No horizon appears in acquiescence, only a kind of despair. A horizon does appear, however, in living out of truthfulness. It is the very horizon of blessedness, a well-being not simply in being poor but in being on the way with the poor, as in the words "chose to be poor," a blessedness that comes from choosing to be on the journey with the poor, from taking their road wherever it leads.

Seeing with the heart and being on the journey with the poor, that is what I see in the blind man and the woman who was poor. That is what I see also in our procession that night from the Church of the Poor Devil. Seeing with the heart has to do with the goal; being on the journey has to do with the way. Here is where Marx's formula comes true, "from each according to his ability, to each according to his needs." If I am willing to be on the journey with the poor, I am willing to give according to my ability and to receive according to my needs, and if I am willing to give and to receive, my heart is open and the eyes of my heart are open. It is the willingness that makes the difference, the choosing as in "Jesus Christ chose to be poor." It is like Solomon's choice, asking for "an understanding mind"[21] rather than for long life or riches or the lives of his enemies. If I choose seeing with the heart over all other things, I am taking the way of heart's desire, I am joining the poor on their journey toward "eternal vision."

It is a choice, seeing with the heart. Before I make it or am able to make it, I am inclined to see everyone and everything in terms of my own needs. I come to see with my heart by going to the heart of deprivation, like the blind man and the woman who was poor, by entering into the experience of lack and loss and letting go. The experience of lack is one of being *bereft* of things that belong to happiness like hope and peace and friendship and insight. The experience of loss, on the other hand, is one of being *bereaved* of a person who belongs to your life. Together the two constitute the heart of deprivation. What is more, there is a link between them. When you lose a person you love, you lose what Scripture calls "the delight of your eyes"—"Son of man, behold, I am about to take the delight of your eyes away from you at a stroke."[22] It is the experience of letting go then that transfigures that of deprivation and opens the eyes of your heart, letting go of the happiness you lack, letting go of the person you have lost.

There is a transfiguration like that, really a "death and transfiguration," in the lives of the poor and the hungry and the sorrowful and the outcast. That is what I was seeing that night, I believe, when I saw people's faces illumined by the candlelight. Passing over to them, entering into their lives, joining them on their journey, I am beginning already to give according to my ability. Coming back to myself, seeing my own experience in the light of their death and transfiguration, I am beginning to receive according to my needs. Here the giving and receiving is only a way, it is true, not a classless society. I have to acknowledge that it is only a way, if I am to be truthful to misery. Still, to act upon that truthfulness, I must go ahead and follow the way and see where it is leading.

"She will see God," Sonia says of her murdered friend in Dostoevsky's *Crime and Punishment*. "Yes . . . she was good . . . she used to come . . . not often . . . she couldn't. . . . We used to read together and . . . talk. She will see God."[23] Sonia is answering the question, "Were you friends?" but she is telling of the way, as I am calling it, the giving and the receiving, and how it leads to the goal, "eternal vision." When you are sharing as she was doing with her friend, living clear down in your heart, you are able to give according to your ability and receive according to your needs. I wonder if it is even possible to share so fully under the sign of human needs without sharing, as these friends were doing, under the sign of heart's desire. If I take Marx's formula as he meant it, "From each . . . to each . . . " describes a classless society, and "only then," as he says there, when the class struggle has been brought to its consummation, will it be possible to give according to our ability and receive according to our needs. If I use the formula, as I am doing, to describe a way rather than a goal, I seem to be describing a way that is impossible unless we go all the way and give and receive according to our heart's desire.

It is here, where the impossible becomes possible, that we come upon "the awful grace of God." In retrospect God appears to be at work all through human suffering, but what God is doing appears to be "grace" (*charis* is the word Aeschylus is using) only when wisdom comes of suffering, when we come to know the heart, and when we begin to act upon wisdom, to give and to receive according to our heart's desire. At first what God is doing in human suffering appears "awful" indeed but not yet gracious except in moments of joy. I wondered how it is possible to be joyful in the midst of misery. I asked a sister who had spent her life working among the poor of Manaus. "Yes," she said to my observation that they seemed to be happy, "they can be sad for a day, but they can't hold on to sadness."

I don't think she meant they are oblivious, forgetting sadness in the immediacy of the present, or unaware, not even perceiving and understanding the loss in their lives. Rather they have a way of letting go of sadness. They live lives of joy and sorrow, and they feel the sorrow without holding on to it, and so they come to joy. It is the first movement of a journey. When you go through life without holding on to it, without holding on to the things you lose, without holding on even to your sorrow at losing them, you are on your way to the sources of life. I think of the scene I saw on the riverboat, the people from the hammocks throwing clothes into the water for the people in the canoes while shouting and cheering and laughing. There was joy in sharing life, in letting go of things. Those words, "From each according to his ability, to each according to his needs," seemed to come true. And yet, as I think about it now in the light of what I am calling "truthfulness to misery," I can see that those words came true only as in an image. I was seeing an image of giving and receiving according to our heart's desire and not yet the reality. Something more is needed, an insight into image and an acting upon insight, for the image to come true.

An awakening is needed, a *conscientizacāo* as it is called,[24] but one that reaches all the way to heart's desire, I would say, and not just to human needs. It does have to reach to human needs, really to our abilities and our needs, for the giving and the receiving to be in accord with them, but it has to reach to our heart's desire, I believe, for there to be a giving and a receiving. When I awaken to my own needs, I become aware of my need for other human beings, my inability to take care of myself. When I awaken to the needs of others, on the other hand, I become aware of my ability to take care of others. When I awaken then to my heart's desire, I become consciously willing to receive, and when I awaken to the heart's desire in others, I become consciously willing to give, realizing how we are desirous of "being recognized, at least by those nearest to us, in the reality that we ourselves do not know, but at best can only live."

Recognition is the heart of giving and receiving. If I recognize another person but am not recognized, I become a slave, and if I am recognized but do not recognize, I become a master, according to Hegel,[25] but if we recognize one another, slavery is abolished or else we become servants of one another, taking care of each other. The recognition has to reach all the way to heart's desire, though, to "the reality that we ourselves do not know, but at best can only live." It is like recognizing a face. When I recognize the face of another person, I not only see but I remember: the recognition is the seeing of a remembered face. It is that way in recognizing another in the reality of the heart's desire too: I not only perceive the other but I remember—I remember my own deepest longing. It is in the light of my own longing that I recognize that of the other. Still, it is in seeing and recognizing the other that my own comes to mind, and it is in being seen and being recognized that I come to know it. Knowledge is acknowledgment.

"The way of man is not in himself"

What if recognition is not forthcoming? Is it possible to forgo it? "This renunciation of recognition will never become possible," Max Frisch says, "without a certitude that our life is directed by a suprahuman authority, without at least the passionate hope that such an authority exists."[26] We can forgo being recognized by others, that is, if we are confident of being recognized by God in our own deepest reality. There is a kind of bliss in being accepted by God that is comparable only to the bliss that is experienced in pure affection. A deep joy is felt in pure affection, in the joyous movement into relatedness with another, in delight at the very thought of the other. A deep joy can be felt also in divine acceptance, in the sense of God drawing near, in the thought of being known to God and being loved by God. If we are confident of God's knowledge and love, it will be because we are confident "that our life is directed by a suprahuman authority." The confidence arises from a sense of being led by God step by step on our journey in time. Or if we are not confident and not surefooted on our journey, we may yet have "the passionate hope that such an authority exists" and in that hope we may be able to trust what lights we do receive along the way.

There was something of that "passionate hope," even that "certitude," in the festival at the Church of the Poor Devil and in our procession at night, as if we were acting out that image of being led by God on a journey in time. It is true, a festival like that of the Poor Devil can seem an image rather of going in circles, and the way it points to can seem a way that goes nowhere. A yearly festival is indeed like the earth's revolving around the sun: the yearly motion of the earth can be seen in the round of the seasons, but the sun's way is hidden. There is a way in interstellar space, nevertheless, along which the solar system is traveling, and it turns the earth's circling into a spiral. So too in the festival of the Poor Devil, I believe, there is a way that is hidden, that is actually going somewhere. Where it is going begins to appear if we act upon that "passionate hope," if we live consciously out of that sense of being on a journey in time.

"I know, O Lord, that the way of man is not in himself," the prophet Jeremiah says, "that it is not in man who walks to direct his steps."[27] And yet God can lead us by our heart's desire and even by our needs. In a festival like that of the Poor Devil the way of relating with God is very elemental. Needs that have been felt and met during the course of the year, that is what you see expressed in the procession of Santo Antonio—some miles south, in the procession at Borba, you see people carrying images of prayers that have been answered, one carrying a model of a foot that has been healed, another carrying one of a head cured of persistent headaches. The way of relating with one another is elemental too. There is a sharing in needs and an understanding of each other's needs and a sharing in joy at needs being met. Coming to the festival with my own way of gaining and sharing insight, I found myself looking for something more than the meeting of needs, "more" as in the saying "we know more than we can tell,"[28] and there is something more, I could see, although it is in relation to needs. There is a knowing of human beings in their needs, an understanding of the human situation, and there is a knowing of God in the meeting of needs, a seeing of meaning in the course of human events. Here then is a way of heart's desire, in knowing human beings and in knowing God, "that I may know me, that I may know thee,"[29] though it be in needs and the meeting of needs.

Speaking of those words of Jeremiah, "the way of man is not in himself," Loren Eiseley says he would add, " 'the way' only lies through man and has to be sought beyond him."[30] Thinking of people knowing one another in their needs and knowing God in the meeting of their needs, I would say that too, meaning human needs, however, when I say "through man" and heart's desire when I say "beyond him." Let me see if I can trace a way through needs and the meeting of needs to something like "eternal vision," to knowing and being known.

If I start with needs and go to knowing, I find I am moving from one focus of feeling to another. The feeling surrounding needs and the meeting of needs is feeling for the things of life, what Yeats calls "primary emotion," while the feeling sur-

rounding the knowing of people in their needs and the know-
ing of God in the meeting of needs is feeling for a relationship
to the things of life, what Yeats calls "antithetical emotion."
When there is feeling only for the things themselves, "man is
so sunk in Fate, in life, that there is no reflection, no experi-
ence," Yeats says, "because that which reflects, that which
acquires experience, has been drowned." When there is no
feeling for relationship, "man cannot think of himself as sepa-
rate from that which he sees with the bodily eye or in the
mind's eye. He neither loves nor hates though he may be in
hatred or in love."[31] A great change occurs, if that is true,
when we go from needs to knowing, we come into reflection
and experience, we become able to distinguish ourselves from
what we see, we become capable of love.

I can see that change in the diary *Child of the Dark*, how the
woman who wrote it comes into reflection and experience in
the very act of writing itself, how she becomes able to distin-
guish herself from what she sees in the *favela*, how she becomes
capable of loving and hating and not just being in love or in
hatred. Her reading and writing, since she has had two years
of schooling, sets her apart from others in the *favela*, to be sure,
and becomes her main source of comfort and light in her
misery. The things she is describing, nevertheless, are the
common events in the lives of people living in poverty, and the
feelings surrounding them are the common feelings. If she
differs from the others, if she emerges from the *favela* even
before she actually leaves, it is because she describes the
common things and the common feelings, because she writes
about them in her diary, because she enters into a conscious
relationship with them.

When I try to pass over to her, I find I am closer to the
feelings she has in writing her diary than to the feelings she
has in living her life. That is because I am coming to her from
the experience of being on a personal journey and keeping at
times a log of my journey in a diary. What I have to learn from

her, though, is contained above all in the feelings she has in living her life. It is one thing to enter into her joy and another to enter into her sadness. "In the old days I sang," she says in the last part of her diary. "Now I've stopped singing, because the happiness has given way to a sadness that ages the heart."[32] When I enter into her joy, as when she says in the first part of her diary, "I am very happy. I sing every morning. I'm like the birds who sing only in the morning because in the morning I'm always happy," I am drawn into her feelings from a desire to participate in the joy, to find that same joy myself. When I enter into her sadness, though, "a sadness that ages the heart," I am dismayed, I am deterred by a fear of being caught up in a sadness that will age my own heart. Then I realize I have known all along there is such sadness but have looked away from it.

I cannot enter into the joy, it seems, without entering also into the sadness. The joy may be that of pure affection, the affection she feels for her three children. I think of Rouault's engraving of mother and child with the title, "It would be so sweet to love."[33] Or it may be that other form of deep joy, the blessedness of being accepted by God. "The first thing I do is open the window and think about heaven," she says when she is talking about singing every morning. Or it may be a combination of the two, the joy of pure affection opening her heart to that of acceptance by God, the sweetness of love enabling her to "open the window and think about heaven." How is it possible for such joy to give way to sadness?

"It would be so sweet to love (*il serait si doux d'aimer*)," Rouault's words, reveal the vulnerable place in the joy, the place where sadness can enter, especially the words in the conditional, "it would be (*il serait*)." There are times when it *is* so sweet to love, when you are absorbed in pure affection, and there are times when it *would be* so sweet to love, when there is pure affection but you cannot lose yourself in it, times when there is a wistfulness, a yearning for return to what seems an irrecoverable condition. The bitterness of a life of poverty can take away the sweetness of love. It is like having a bitter taste in your mouth and not being able to taste the sweetness of what you are eating. The sweetness is there, the pure affection is there, but because of the bitter taste in your mouth, the bitter taste of poverty, you are not able to taste the sweetness. So too, if pure affection is your doorway to the feeling of being accepted by God, you are not able to taste that sweetness either, you are not able to "taste and see that the Lord is good."[34] That is what I see as I enter into this woman's sadness. "Laugh, child. Life is beautiful," she quotes from a Brazilian poet. But then she changes it to "Cry, child. Life is bitter."[35] She says this to herself, looking at her youngest child, who is smiling. It is like the mother and child in Rouault's engraving, the child seeing only the mother but the mother seeing life and its bitterness.

Writing about her joy and her sadness in her diary, she turns it into experience and reflection. It is already experience and reflection to some extent: that is the difference between the mother and the child. Writing it down, though, makes the experience more conscious and the reflection more deliberate. If her sadness is "a sadness that ages the heart," as she says, that is not because she writes about it. Rather the aging of the heart is the process Aeschylus is talking about when he speaks of "wisdom" that comes "by the awful grace of God." The aging of the heart does not occur in wakeful consciousness but "drop, drop—in our sleep" as "upon the heart sorrow falls, memory's pain." It does not take place by our own choice but "against our very will, even in our own despite." What happens in writing is that the unconscious process becomes conscious, the unwilling change becomes willing, the aging of the heart becomes an articulate wisdom.

It is still possible to let go of sadness even if it ages the heart, even if you record it as this woman does in her diary. A few days after she speaks of "a sadness that ages the heart" she is able to say again, "Today I am happy."[36] The letting go comes of the wisdom itself. It is wise to let go of sadness and enter again into joy. Although she has said "Cry, child. Life is bitter," and has cried herself and has not forgotten the bitterness of life, she is able to let go of sorrowing and let herself enjoy the things of life, enjoy simply having something to eat ("nowadays when a poor man eats meat he keeps smiling stupidly"). It is not that having something to eat is able by itself to dispel her sadness. Rather she has to let go of sadness in order to feel joy. Letting go is a releasing and a being released, as in the Shaker song, " 'Tis the gift to be simple, 'tis the gift to be free."[37] It is something that comes "by the awful grace of God."

To be simple, to be free, I believe, one has to come to a letting go that is conscious and willing. That is something that happens for her only later, after she has escaped from poverty and is being forced to return to it, when she says, "One can live better when one is poor than when one is rich," when she sees poverty in terms of Christ who "chose to be poor." When she is writing her diary, she is able to turn misery into experience and reflection, to differentiate herself from her lot in life and from the misery she sees in the *favela*, to take a conscious stance toward misery and reject it. Later, when she is about to return to poverty, she does not change her No into a Yes to misery. Rather her Yes, if I understand her rightly, is to letting go. It is to the blessedness of pure affection, of acceptance by God. It is to being simple, to being free, to giving and receiving according to her heart's desire.

"She died a pauper in 1977."[38] That is the end of her story as we know it from the outside. It seems to make Marx's point that giving according to our ability and receiving according to our needs will never come about without a change in "the ensemble of the social relations." All that is possible without a new society is a willingness to give and to receive. "We know that the new form of social production, to achieve the good

life," he says, "needs only *new men*."[39] Yet new men and
women do come about through the willingness to give and to
receive, through the process that takes place in the life of this
woman as she comes to consciousness and willingness. She
becomes a new person. She comes first to consciousness, writ-
ing her diary, and then later on to willingness, joining the poor
on their journey with Christ who "chose to be poor." That
consciousness and willingness is a way, it seems to me, though
it hasn't yet brought about the new society. What it brings
about is new men and women, and that must be the true goal
of the journey of the poor, not just a new society for those who
live in a future age but new men and women all along the way
in time.

Consciousness and willingness do make new men and
women, do change the relationship of people to existing soci-
ety and thus do prepare the way for a new society, but only
because there is something going on in people already that can
become conscious and willing, a joy and a sorrow that are a
learning of the heart. It is what is going on prior to con-
sciousness and willingness that makes the journey of the poor,
the course of life from birth to death, to be sure, like the daily
course of the sun across the sky, but something more, an
experience that is extended by the conjoining of many lives
and that is concentrated by pain. It is the distilling of wisdom
upon the heart. When it becomes conscious and willing, the
wisdom becomes a conscious truthfulness to joy and misery, a
knowing of one another's hearts, and being on the journey
becomes a willing consent to knowing and being known, to
understanding and being understood.

Before it becomes conscious understanding, the journey of
the poor is memory, the memory of one life like that of the
woman keeping her diary and yet the memory of many lives
like those of the many whose lives were intertwined with hers.
As I enter into that pool of memory, I realize that my own life
too has emerged from a matrix of many lives, that my personal

existence has come about with my emergence as an individual. When the memory becomes experience and reflection, as it did for the woman recording it in her diary, the conscious individual emerges and is set over and against the circumstances of life. Here is where the relationship of a person to existing society is changed. Consciousness comes with literacy somewhat as history comes with the invention of writing. Although things happened and stories were told during prehistoric times, a new awareness came with writing and the recording of events, history was being recorded and so was being made. Something similar seems to come of literacy when it is put to use. Before she kept her diary things were happening for the woman in the *favela* and she no doubt told others about them. After she began keeping her diary, though, she came to a new awareness of what was happening in her life, both of the joy and of the sorrow. It was not literacy by itself that made the difference, her two years of schooling as a child, but her putting it to use in keeping a diary. As you come to consciousness of what is happening in your life, of your joy and your sorrow, you can begin living out of your consciousness, you can begin living clear down in your heart.

Understanding then is not just memory become experience and reflection. It is living clear down in your heart. It comes with the willingness to know and be known, to understand and be understood. If you are not poor, consciousness itself is a matter of willingness. "The unconscious," it has been said, "is the direction we are not looking."[40] I have to be willing to look in the direction of misery to become conscious of it. If you are poor like the woman in the *favela*, consciousness is one thing and willingness is another. Still, in the end willingness even then is a willingness to look in the direction of misery. Although she was forced back into poverty, after the publication of her diary had bought her a few years of escape, she was able nonetheless to come to a kind of willingness to be on the journey with the poor. If I too join the poor on their journey, I come to a new consciousness and a new willingness myself. It is by way of consciousness and willingness that I join them, the willingness making the consciousness possible.

Now if I do join them, if I do enter into the conjoining of lives and the pain, I come upon an answer to my initial question, *Which is the way?* I have gone, looking for the way, from people relating to one another, giving and receiving, to people relating to themselves, coming to consciousness and willingness. My question comes out of a story Walter de la Mare tells of meeting an otherworldly stranger one evening in a country churchyard. The stranger poses the question to him, asking as it seems for some common way, thinking maybe of the way from life to death, the original meaning of "the way of all flesh."[41] *Which is yours?* the stranger asks him when he shakes his head at the first question, asking this time it seems for a personal way. My own question has changed too from "Which is the way?" asking about the journey of the poor to "Which is yours?" asking myself about my own consciousness of the journey and my own willingness to be with the poor. When he is shown "the human road," the road leading from the churchyard to town, the otherworldly stranger seems dismayed, "the astonishment and dread in the strange face seemed to deepen," and when de la Mare turns again to speak with him he is gone.[42] Evidently the human road is not his way. Is it mine?

Yes, if I may understand the human road in terms of my own way of gaining and sharing insight, if I may see the human road as a way of following our heart's desire. For me there is an image here, that of the human road, and an insight into the image, the insight that comes with knowing and being known in our deepest longing, with living clear down in our heart. If the human road were simply "the way of all flesh," the course or passage from life to death, the way people live and suffer and die, I think I would feel only "astonishment and dread" like the otherworldly stranger in de la Mare's story who evidently "sees in it some disaster not anticipated by ourselves."[43] The disaster would be to live only for our needs and not for our heart's desire. If I may see the human road as the way of naked humanity, however, the way of the poor, the way taken by Christ, then I can see it as a way not simply of living and dying but of knowing and loving.

It is true, joining the poor on their journey means joining them also in their struggle for emergence. If the conjoining of lives in coming to light out of the darkness of pain is a journey, a voyage of discovery, it is also a struggle, a fight for recognition in a conflict of masters and slaves. The light of discovery and the light of recognition are one and the same. *The way is that of knowing and being known in our naked humanity.* I think of the nakedness of Jesus upon the cross. "When you have lifted up the Son of man," Jesus says in the Gospel of John, "then you will know that I am."[44] When you have lifted me up on the cross, he is saying, then you will know that I am as Moses heard God say I AM from the burning bush.[45] Something like this happens also when the poor emerge in their naked humanity, it seems, the great I AM of God is revealed in them. We know and are known in our naked humanity; we say, "I am," and God says I AM in us.

God is revealed in our naked humanity because our heart's desire is revealed. I think of Al-Hallaj the mystic and martyr saying, "I want to be eternally young in Him, eternally filled with desire, for He is the Essential Desire." In our suffering our heart's desire comes to light. "I am willing to be accused, hung up for all to see, to have light squeezed from my aging darkness, by God," he says, thinking of his approaching death on the gibbet at the hands of his enemies. "His spark, eternal for me, may it flash in my heart and I be His darkness."[46] That is what comes to pass in Jesus lifted up on the cross, I believe, and Hallaj is looking to Jesus as his original, and that is what is coming to pass again and again, it seems, as people emerge in their naked humanity. It is still true, what Jeremiah said, "that the way of man is not in himself, that it is not in man who walks to direct his steps." For if we are acting upon the insights that arise out of suffering, then the steps we are to take are being revealed to us one after another as we go from one insight to another. At the same time, " 'the way' only lies through man and has to be sought beyond him." For if the insights arise out of suffering, then they are arising out of our own journey through the darkness of our pain into the light of our heart's desire.

I don't mean that God is reducible to our longing, that the way of man is one of suffering rather than of praxis, of undergoing rather than of doing, that Christ is only a prototype of man. I mean rather that we are connected with God by our longing, that the praxis of the way is one of acting upon insight into suffering, that we come to the goal by enacting our relationship with Christ.

"It happens at times that the way is beautiful,"[47] Rouault writes beneath one of his engravings, showing a family on shore and a boat in the foreground and a curving horizon in the background. The beauty appears in moments of joy, in the blessedness of pure affection and of acceptance by God. There is something in moments of sadness as well, if the way is that taken by Christ, even in "a sadness that ages the heart." Walking the human road with the thought of Christ walking it is actually like doing what Rouault himself is doing, working on his engravings, doing them over and over again, setting the images of suffering humanity side by side with those of Christ. He works in a kind of twilight, and yet a radiance begins to show. It becomes a visible light in his later paintings. "I spent my life painting twilights," he explained. "I ought to have the right now to paint the dawn."[48] We too can spend our lives painting twilights, living over and over again the scenes of human suffering, gaining insight by setting them side by side with images of Christ's suffering, but we can be led, insight by insight, to painting the dawn, to living in the light of Jesus risen from the dead.

There is a green flash, a momentary green appearance of

the uppermost part of the sun's disk, that occurs when the sun sinks below or rises above the horizon. There is an insight too, a momentary illumination of the human road, that occurs when the heart's desire is kindled in response to the prospect of death or the hope of resurrection. It is an insight that occurs again and again because the heart is kindled again and again, but it is always a new insight because we are always at a different point in our journey along the human road. Acting upon this insight is like acting upon a principle of giving according to our ability and receiving according to our needs, and acting upon it gives it a certain reality even without the reality of a classless society. Because it is insight, though, and not really a principle, what giving and receiving mean, what ability and needs mean looks different at each different stage of our long night's journey into day.

"Eternal vision," if our recurring insight is its substance, must mean seeing what God sees, seeing into the darkness of the human heart, and seeing God by seeing the flash in that darkness when the heart is kindled. "His spark, eternal for me, may it flash in my heart and I be His darkness." That is what it must mean to know and be known in our naked humanity. God's spark, eternal for us, flashes in our heart and we become God's darkness, and we come to know and be known in our heart's longing. Before God's spark flashes, all we know is our naked mortality. After it flashes in our heart, we come to know the power of resurrection, even though we are still on this side of death. In that power, even apart from a classless society, we can give and receive. In that power, even before death and the ending of time, we can live.

FOUR

The Person
and the Vision

"Now that I can see it all as from a lonely hilltop," Black Elk says of his life, "I know it was the story of a mighty vision given to a man too weak to use it."[1] Passing over, as I have been doing, to our journey together in time, to the religion of the poor, to the way that leads through human misery to heart's desire, I seem to be entering like him into "a mighty vision." Coming back again, however, to my own journey in life, to personal religion, to my own particular way, I seem to be coming back to "a man too weak to use it."

I see in the vision something like a great migration of peoples, something that occurs not in one time or from one place as a starting point but at many times and in many places with many starts and stops, a great journey in which we are all participants to one degree or another, conscious or unconscious, willing or unwilling, but one that is visible only in loosely connected episodes. We are like migratory birds flying

from breeding to wintering areas or from wintering to breed-
ing areas, or like migratory laborers traveling from one area to
another in search of work where labor is seasonal, or like
immigrants moving from one country or region or place to
settle in another. There is something we are trying to reach
like the feeding or breeding grounds or the work or the new
place to live, and there is something we are trying to get away
from, the place or the situation where we have been and its
lack of prospect. Religion is the expression of both of these
things, our heart's desire and the situation we have been living
in, and the way is a route from the one to the other, from the
human situation to the heart's desire. Because the journey
goes on with many starts and stops, though, we have to keep
drawing a line on the map from the one point to the other,
from where we actually are to where we long to be. We are
always making the journey, expressing our situation and our
longing, and finding the way. So the vision is a recurrent
vision, like a recurrent dream.

My own journey in life, when I come back to it, when I
awaken, as it were, from this vision, though it seems only a
very small episode in time, seems somehow to encompass the
larger journey within itself, for my passing over to our journey
together has now become a part of my own adventure. I come
back indeed with the feelings of the larger journey, the joy and
the sorrow, and I know I have been changed by them. I know
"misery is real"[2] as the woman of the *favela* said, and I wonder
what I am to do about it. Personal religion has been for me an
expression of my own situation in life, my own loneliness, and of
my own heart's desire, the longing in my loneliness. Now I see
the situation of others, especially that of the poor, and I see how
my longing is connected with their longing. Yet what am I to do
about the misery of the poor? Here is where "a mighty vision"
has been "given to a man too weak to use it," unless I can do
something about it simply by giving expression to what I see.

"What can I know? What should I do? What may I hope?"[3]
Kant's three questions can guide me here. What I can know

about people and their longing and their way is what I can learn from passing over to them and coming back to myself, and what I should do, it seems, is just that, pass over and come back, then give expression to whatever I find. What I may hope is to kindle a light in the darkness of the human situation. Let me see what happens to a person in passing over, in coming to a vision, and what happens in coming back, in returning to oneself and putting the vision to use.

Coming to a Vision

When I compare what I am seeing, a great journey in time, with what Marx saw, a continual struggle of classes ("the history of all hitherto existing society is the history of class struggles"),[4] I wonder if there is something missing in my vision, if I have the same blind spot that Yeats found in Shelley who "lacked the Vision of Evil, could not conceive of the world as a continual conflict."[5] On the other hand, maybe the struggle can be seen as a part of the journey, as in Black Elk's vision who saw his people walking two roads, a red one, "the road of good," and a black, "a fearful road, a road of troubles and war."[6] The real question is *Who can see the human road?* One who sees human misery may come to a revolutionary vision of human society and its future; one who sees the heart's longing may come to a critical vision of society and a utopian vision of the consummation of human affairs; but one who sees both human misery and the heart's longing without taking either one of them for an illusion may come, I believe, to a vision of the human road.

If I see the circumstances of the poor, the dimensions of human misery, but take the heart's longing for an illusion, a wishful hope that comes from a religious acceptance of the limits imposed by circumstances, from accepting poverty and deprivation as the "will of God," then I will see real hope only in a struggle against those circumstances, and against ruling classes who impose the limits on others, and against what purports to be the "will of God." Take away the acceptance of poverty and deprivation and the true heart's desire will emerge, I will be convinced, a desire to arise out of a wretched condition, a simple desire to be happy. If I see substance in the heart's longing, on the contrary, in the desire to see God, but take human misery for an illusion, a wishful discontent that comes from seeing some have what others do not have, from believing unhappiness is due to not having and happiness will come with having, then I will be inclined to conclude, like Leon Bloy in *The Woman Who Was Poor*, "There is only one misery, and that is—not to be saints."[7] Take away the illusion that having will make us happy and the true heart's desire will emerge, I will be convinced, a desire for the happiness that comes fron knowing you are fulfilling the will of God, from walking simply with God.

If I see both human misery and the heart's longing, however, and do not take either one for an illusion, if I see that there really is misery and that it is want and suffering due to the conditions of life, if I see that there really is a yearning of the heart and that it cannot be satisfied with anything less than God, then I can see how human misery determines the starting point and the heart's longing determines the goal of a great journey in time. It is a journey that I can join wherever I am and wherever we are along the human road. To actually see the human road, though, I have to see where we are in terms of human misery and where we are going in terms of the heart's longing. I have to participate in the heart's longing, something that comes with letting my own heart be kindled, and I have to participate also in human misery, something that comes with letting myself feel my connection with people who live in want and suffering.

I have to enter upon something like a "vision quest," the solitary vigil an American Indian boy keeps to seek spiritual power and learn the identity of his guardian spirit. The solitary vigil for me is a waiting for the kindling of my heart and the feeling of my connection with the poor, a waiting for insight into the human road. There is power whenever insight comes, and there is a sense of being led, of the God who is Spirit guarding and guiding me along the way. Let me try to reenact the vigil and see how it leads into the vision.

My heart is kindled when I think of being on an adventure in time, and I come to a feeling of connection with the poor when I think of being with them on the adventure. It is true, I cannot produce the kindling of the heart or the feeling of connection at will. They come to me in the memory of actual experiences of the adventure, a riverboat voyage, a chapel, a procession at night. Whenever I bring the experiences to mind, though, my heart is rekindled and I feel again the connection, and I can almost descry the road ahead. I seem to see something like an afterglow, a reillumination of mountains after the summits have passed into shadow at sunset, a reddish glow where darkness has fallen. I almost see what I desire to see, almost know what I desire to know of the human journey. To actually see, to actually know, I have to take the experiences as images of the journey as a whole and come to an insight into the images. I have to go to the mind and heart of the adventure.

I find that the human road is always "the road past the view,"[8] a winding road that disappears over the horizon or into the mountains. It is a road that can be seen ahead but then goes on into the unknown. That is because we do not simply choose it. We discover it as we go. It is like a river we follow upstream leading us back to its source out of sight in the mountains, or like the inner space of a chapel full of the seen and also the unseen, or like a procession at night with candles where light is surrounded by darkness. "From a certain point onward there is no longer any turning back," Kafka says. "That is the point that must be reached."[9] There is a point like that on the human road whether we see it as a road of life leading to the sources of life or a road of love leading to the heart's desire or a road of knowledge leading to "eternal vision." The point of no return is always a point ahead, between where we are and where we are going, where the road disappears.

On the road leading to the sources of life the intervening point of no return is the point of death. That is the irony of our journey together in time, that we each die along the way. Of what significance is the journey for us, we can wonder, if we must each die before it comes to its goal? One answer is to say we each have our own purpose in being on the journey. There is the overall purpose of the journey, to come to the sources of life, and there is the particular purpose of each individual, something that can be accomplished in a lifetime. I can have a purpose of my own apart from that of the journey as a whole, if I choose my way in life, if I give my life a goal. That is the secret of a life, William Carlos Williams says in the preface to his autobiography:

> I am extremely sexual in my desires: I carry them everywhere
> and at all times. I think that from that arises the drive which
> empowers us all. Given that drive, a man does with it what his
> mind directs. In the manner in which he directs that power lies
> his secret.[10]

There is a direction in the heart's longing, nevertheless, that is there before any direction of our own choosing. I find it if I let myself be led by insight, discovering my way step by step. I find myself moving toward the universal goal, toward the sources of life. And if I make the universal purpose my own conscious and deliberate purpose, if I make it my "secret," I become like Eve seeking the lost paradise in Moody's *Death of Eve*, "who loves as wide as life, though deep as death."[11] I do come to the goal then, though I die along the way.

I come to the goal, to the sources of life, by loving "as wide as life," by letting the road of life become for me the road of love. When Eve turns again toward the lost paradise in Moody's play, after years of living in fear and numbness, she comes to life again and takes courage. "I know not what is in me!" she says. "I am changed from all I was. Or am I back-returned through life's deep changes to my changeless self?"[12] It is as if she finds the sources of life simply by daring to turn toward them. There is still a journey to make, to be sure, to find Cain and travel with him, retracing his wanderings, until she comes again to Eden. Yet in some way she comes to the journey's end as soon as she sets her mind on making it. "Thy soul is back-returned," she is told, "through life's sad changes to the joy it was when first it soared into the new-made light."[13] That is what happens for me when I turn toward the sources of life, when I let the universal heart's longing be my own heart's desire. I come to my true self, for the universal longing is indeed my heart's desire, and I recover my soul, for my fear and numbness are swallowed up in the kindling of my heart.

I still must die along the way. That is where the truth of human misery touches my life, even if I do not actually live in poverty. "You can't be any poorer than dead,"[14] Flannery O'Connor says in the title of one of her stories, for in death you have to let go of everyone and everything. If I recognize that truth, without thereby taking the heart's longing and the sources of life for an illusion, then the road of life and love becomes for me the road of knowledge. And if I am still willing to walk the road, knowing that, I begin to love "as deep as death." I become like Eve in Moody's poem "The Death of Eve,"[15] the forerunner of his play, where she actually comes again to the garden of paradise and sings a song to God and then dies. Or better, since I have not actually died, I become like her in Moody's play where she sees the angel of death and knows she is going to die but determines to go ahead "on that fearful way that I must go, and that I haste to go ere darkness falls forever."[16] If I take both the sources of life and the utter poverty of death for reality, that is, and am willing to walk the "fearful way" that leads through utter poverty to inexhaustible richness, then I am walking like Eve and Cain "into the gaze and silence of the Lord," into a being seen that is a seeing and into a being heard that is a hearing. I am walking into "eternal vision," as we sang in the chapel of the Poor Devil, into a being known that is a knowing.

Knowing comes of loving. Knowing and loving are not simply things of life but are the two basic modes of relating to the things. Knowledge consists of taking the things into oneself—what I know of them I have within me—while love consists of going out to the things themselves, to the persons and the situations that belong to my life. Loving "as wide as life, though deep as death," if my own road in life leads into the human road, means simply being willing to walk my road to the end. And knowing comes of living when I have the courage to think the thought through to the end, when I am willing to walk the human road to the end also in thought.

It is here, thinking the thought through to the end, that I come to the point where the road disappears from my view. Although I know I will die someday, I do not know when that day will be. Entering into that uncertainty about death, I enter upon an adventure in search of life. I remember the days of uncertainty before our voyage upriver, when I was unsure of finding passage on the riverboat, and then the richness of life I found on the voyage itself after being prepared by such a thirst for it. The entries in my diary speak of thirst: "Thirsty today (don't dare drink the water here), readings on thirst today too (Psalm 63, John 7:37–39), a physical and a spiritual thirst." I was like Bloy's "woman who was poor" who was "athirst for Life," who was "dying of the longing to live," and who was told by a mysterious priest from the desert that she should pray to Eve, "mother of all living," and that he would be praying for her too "when you are in the midst of the flames."[17] Now, as I recall all this and try to complete in thought our voyage to the sources of life, to think it through to the end, I feel more like a pilgrim Bloy describes who may be Bloy himself, who spends his life searching for the lost garden of Eden, and who stops at last in a cemetery of lepers where the tree of life is indeed growing and the Spirit of God walks in the afternoon air.

What I actually found at the end of the voyage, instead of a cemetery of lepers, was the chapel of the Poor Devil, and that became for me the embodiment and expression of the heart's longing. At the time I did not realize the importance of what I had found. There is no mention of the chapel in my diary! It is only now, remembering it and having seen it again, that I realize how it tells, rather differently than a cemetery, of the heart's desire. Bloy's pilgrim found that "the lost paradise is the cemetery, and the only way to recover it is to die."[18] I found that it is a chapel and to recover it is to enter an imaginative space that is full of gods and saints, to let that space become still and empty like the earth in the beginning, and to let the presence of God be felt there like breath stirring the water.

Two years after my first visit to the chapel, I decided I had to go back again, to find out who the Poor Devil was and to be there for the festival when the chapel was open. I went back this time to find the tree of knowledge as well as the tree of life. There is something essential to be learned, I believed, from the conjunction of human misery and the heart's longing that is to be found in the religion of the poor. Bloy's "woman who was poor" learned "that there is only one way of making contact with God, and that this way, for a woman especially, is Poverty."[19] That goes with his having her say, "There is only one misery, and that is—not to be saints." Poverty for Bloy as a way is the nakedness and simplicity of following the heart's desire. If poverty is also real misery, though, as the woman of the *favela* said, the real woman who was poor, then it is a way of contacting God only if we acknowledge the misery, only if we acknowledge the human needs that are unfulfilled. And if we do acknowledge human misery, then following the heart's desire comes to mean taking "the road past the view," taking a road that leads out of the human situation we know.

It is true, the point where the road disappears from my view is the point of death, and so it can seem "the lost paradise is the cemetery," as Bloy's pilgrim found, "and the only way to recover it is to die." Yet it is the uncertainty rather than the certainty of death that causes the road to disappear, and it is the uncertainty that brings me to life and sets me on the adventure in search of life. Bloy's pilgrim, when he came to the cemetery of lepers, did not simply die but he "died of love,"[20] and Eve too, when she had returned to the garden of Eden in Moody's poem, died singing a song of freedom to God. There is an element of uncertainty in the entire human situation and in that uncertainty there is room for a human adventure. The uncertainty appears when we set human misery and the heart's longing side by side. When we consider either one of them alone, the problem can seem to contain its own solution, human misery working toward its own reversal and the heart's longing working toward its own fulfillment. When we consider them side by side, however, we come upon a seeming contradiction.

Looking at one side of the contradiction, we can say, as Bloy himself does at first, that poverty "has the power to make human beings feel the burden of the flesh and the deplorable enslavement of the mind"; looking at the contradiction itself, we can say, as he does further on in the story, that "no man has ever been able to say what poverty is"; and looking at the other side of the contradiction, we can say, as he does in the end, that poverty is the "way of making contact with God."[21] Actually his sequence of thought here is telling and shows us three stages we go through in coming to see the human road.

I see first the clash between human misery and the heart's longing, how human misery seems to weigh down the heart's longing by making people feel "the burden of the flesh and the deplorable enslavement of the mind." Passing over into those feelings, I realize I carry the same burden of flesh, the same need for food and clothing and shelter, and live in the same enslavement of mind, the same dependency on money ("the heart of the poor is a black dungeon which must be taken by silver weapons, which only ammunition of money can forge!").[22] The difference is that deprivation has caused the poor to feel the burden and the enslavement. Their situation is a universal one; it is the human situation itself; but poverty causes them to feel the human situation to a degree that others do not. If I enter into their feeling, I feel the heart's longing weighed down by need and dependency, and yet I am a step nearer than I was, it seems, to the heart's realization. I have to find some way, now that I feel it, of becoming free of "the burden of the flesh" and the "enslavement of the mind." I have to find a new relationship to the material conditions of life.

Here I come upon that element of uncertainty in the human situation that allows more than one relationship to material conditions, that allows room for a human adventure. " 'The poor you have always with you,' " Bloy quotes from the Gospel of John. "In the whole abyss of time since that Word," he goes on then to say, "no man has ever been able to say what poverty is."[23] I come here upon something like the "uncertainty principle" in physics. The more precisely you determine the position of a moving particle, according to that principle, the less precisely can you determine its motion, and vice versa the more precisely you determine its motion the less precisely can you determine its position. So too the more exactly you define human misery in terms of the material conditions of life the less exactly can you define the heart's longing—it becomes simply a general longing to be happy and to escape from a wretched situation. And vice versa the more exactly you define the heart's longing as a desire for God the less exactly can you define human misery—it can be a situation that weighs down the heart's longing or it can be, on the contrary, a "way of making contact with God."

It is our relationship to the material conditions of life that decides their significance for us. If I live in subjection to material conditions, then they weigh down my heart's longing. If I live in freedom toward material conditions, then poverty can be a way for me of making contact with God. We are not simply free, however, to choose our relationship. Bloy's "woman who was poor" does not find poverty a way to God until after she has escaped from it for a while and then is plunged back into it again. It is then that she is able to say, "There is only one misery, and that is—not to be saints." And the woman of the *favela* does not find poverty a better way than riches until after she has escaped from the *favela* for a few years and then is being forced back into poverty. It is then that she too concludes, "One can live better when one is poor than when one is rich," and "perhaps that is why Jesus Christ chose to be poor."[24]

A way opens up before us, it seems, only after we have been able to differentiate ourselves from our lot in life and see ourselves otherwise than in the situation of our past. It is then that we are able to see the road of naked humanity leading out of the human situation we know. The contrast here is between the human situation and the human essence. The human situation, for all its universality, includes not only the conditions of human life, material and otherwise, but also the relationship to those conditions in which we have been living. The human essence, on the other hand, our "naked humanity" as I have been calling it, is something that is partially eclipsed in the relation of subjection to death and to the material conditions of life in which we have been living and is revealed for what it is only in a relationship with God. For in living out the heart's longing for God we become free toward death and toward material conditions. Death is not abolished, to be sure, nor is matter abolished, but our relationship with death and with matter is changed.

I see a road leading out of the human situation we know,

therefore, leading out of human misery and in the direction of the heart's longing. It disappears into the mountains, for it leads out of the situation we know and thus out of our present knowledge. I can tell, nevertheless, that it is a road of naked humanity, that it is a living out of the heart's longing for God, and that we walk it in freedom toward death and the material conditions of life. It disappears ahead from view because we discover it as we go, because it leads us out into the unknown, because we die along the way. I can tell, nevertheless, that it leads to "eternal vision," a goal that is far and near, as near to each of us as death itself and as far from all of us as the fulfillment of all life.

Returning to Oneself

I see a vision of a vision, that is, a vision of a road leading into a vision. As I come back to myself now and my own journey in life, I wonder how I am to walk the road and share the vision with others. I wonder too if there is something I can do about the misery of the poor other than share my vision and walk the road myself. "All mysteries which mislead theory to mysticism," Marx says, "find their rational solution in human practice and in the comprehension of this practice."[25] What he is talking about, I think, is the way human misery works toward its own reversal. Yet if I take into account not only the working out of misery but also that of the heart's longing, I come upon an uncertainty, as we saw, rather than an unmystical and unmysterious "comprehension." And now, as I return to myself and ask myself how I am to use my vision, I think of "a mighty vision" and "a man too weak to use it," and I find myself plunged into the uncertainty I have discovered.

When I focus upon misery and define it sharply in terms of the material conditions of life, of having and not having, and let the heart's longing remain relatively undefined, a general longing to escape from misery, then I see my own task like

Marx as one of working with misery working toward its own reversal. People living in want and suffering, if they do not simply resign themselves to their lot, find themselves involved in a struggle to change their lot or in a journey, a sort of migration, moving from the old to a new situation. What I should do, in view of this, is join the poor in their struggle or on their journey, knowing that in joining the poor I am really joining all humanity and working toward the unity of the human race, crossing the barrier between those who have and those who have not. What remains vague and elusive, because the heart's longing is still undefined, is the direction of the struggle or the journey, not the "from" but the "toward," the happy union of people that is to come.

When I focus instead upon the heart's longing and define it in terms of a human relationship with God, and let misery remain undefined except as an experience of unhappiness, then I see my task as one of working with the heart's longing working toward its own fulfillment. The heart's longing can be experienced as joy in the midst of sorrow and as sorrow in the midst of joy, for it is "an unsatisfied desire," as C. S. Lewis says, "which is itself more desirable than any other satisfaction."[26] What I should do, if I look to that joy and sorrow, is let it become a light guiding me on my own journey and, sharing it with others, a light guiding also our journey together in time. What remains obscure, if I focus only upon the heart's longing and leave human misery undefined, is what to do about the material conditions of life, about having and not having, about the misery of the poor. I can become like Bloy drawing back from the work of Rouault, though it was inspired partly by his own work in *The Woman Who Was Poor*,[27] drawing back nevertheless from the unrelieved horror of human misery.

Living in uncertainty without despairing, Kierkegaard's way of living by faith,[28] can be an answer. If I am willing to live in the uncertainty that arises from holding to the truth both of misery and of longing and not despair of the poor emerging or of coming with them to the consummation of their yearning, then one insight after another can come to me out of the sheer uncertainty itself. My task becomes to cast aside fear and despair and act upon whatever insight I have, even if it is only this bifocal correction of our existing vision of the near and the distant.

Before insight comes I am stymied by a lack of focus and of grounding, a lack of focus in what I am doing, trying to alleviate human misery and follow the heart's longing as if I were moving in two different directions at once, and a lack of grounding in what I am feeling about human misery, alternating between hope and despair, and about the heart's longing, alternating between confidence and mistrust. What happens when insight comes is that I see the focus and feel the grounding. Insight comes of actually joining the poor on their journey, as I did on the riverboat, of actually participating in the religion of the poor, as I did at the chapel of the Poor Devil, of actually walking the way with the poor, as I began to do on the night of the festival. I do not see how to act upon the insight, nevertheless, until I return to myself and my own life and see the focus through my own eyes and feel the grounding with my own heart.

Here again I come upon the point of no return, only now it is the point of no return in my own journey in life. "There is a point at which everything becomes simple and there is no longer any question of choice," Hammarskjold says in his diary, "because all you have staked will be lost if you look back. Life's point of no return."[29] It is not that I am unable to return to my own journey or to personal religion or to my own particular way in life. It is rather that my journey has become the journey together, my religion has become that of the poor, and my way has become that of the universal heart's desire. My own road disappears now into the human road. To act, nevertheless, I must travel the journey together as my own journey, live the religion of the poor as personal religion, walk the universal way as my way.

An initial insight is the one that came to me on our river-boat voyage up the Amazon, like Katherine Anne Porter's insight into the image of "the ship of fools," "I am a passenger on that ship."[30] It is the realization that I am on a journey with the rich and the poor to the sources of life. At first it seems nothing much could come of such an insight. When I compare it with Bloy's insight, though, seeing himself as a "pilgrim of the Absolute," and the loneliness he felt at the thought, "when they found out the road I was taking, when it became notorious that I was a man of the Absolute, no one would follow me . . . ,"[31] I can see how in passing over to the journey together I am joining others in a pilgrimage of the Absolute, how I am with others in "the ship of this world on its voyage to eternity." When I come back to myself then, I realize that I am no longer alone on my journey, that I have to let go of a jealous love that wants to be alone with God, that what has happened to me "comes of loving a God whose love cannot be limited to one alone."[32] If I am willing to live now out of a love that cannot be limited to me, and not demand a love that is exclusive, I enter into a new relationship with others and our journey becomes my journey.

A further insight is the one that came to me at the chapel of the Poor Devil, like Simone Weil's insight into Christianity as a religion of slaves, "and I among others."[33] It is the realization that I share the heart's longing that is expressed in the religion of the poor. Here too it can seem that nothing much would come of such an insight. When I think of Marx's insight into the religion of the poor, though, seeing it as "the sigh of the oppressed creature, the heart of a heartless world, and the soul of soulless conditions,"[34] I can see how in passing over to the religion of the poor I am entering into the heart and soul of the poor and sharing in their deepest aspirations. When I return to myself then, if I do not also accept Marx's judgment that religion is an illusion, "the opium of the people," I realize that "the sigh of the oppressed creature" is also my own sigh, "the heart of a heartless world" is also my own heart, and "the soul of soulless conditions" is also my own soul. If I am willing to live out of that heart and soul and to express that sigh myself, I enter into a new relationship with the poor and their religion becomes my religion, like Ruth saying to Naomi, "Your people shall be my people, and your God my God."[35]

Still another insight is the one that came to me in our procession on the night of the festival, like the insight implied in the two questions posed by Walter de la Mare, "Which is the way?" and "Which is yours?"[36] It is the realization that my own road in life leads into the human road. Here again it can seem that such an insight is only a commonplace and is therefore of little consequence. When I compare Marx and Bloy on the poor, though, and see the difference between a poverty in which a person lacks everything that is superfluous and a misery in which a person lacks even what is necessary for a human existence, I can see how misery, as Marx believed, is a point of departure while poverty, as Bloy believed, is a way. I can see how in passing over to the poor and being with them on their way I am entering into a relationship both with misery and with poverty. When I return to myself then, I realize I have learned something about our naked humanity, something about ourselves that will show us the way. If I am willing to live out of that nakedness myself, to know others in their naked humanity, and to be known myself in mine, I enter into a new relationship with humanity and the human road becomes my road, like Christ who "emptied himself,"[37] who could say, thinking of naked humanity, "I am poor."

Those words, "I am poor," Bloy is ready to ascribe to God himself. "When we inquire of God, he replies that it is he who is the poor one—*Ego sum pauper*," Bloy says. "When we inquire not of him, he displays the glory of his riches."[38] I can

see how I am being led to something similar, saying "God has
no essence" and "God is the heart's desire" and "the way is
that of knowing and being known in our naked humanity."
Somehow the existence of human misery side by side with the
heart's longing says something about God. "When we inquire
of God, he replies that it is he who is the poor one"—somehow
that goes with the existence of human misery, and "when we
inquire not of him, he displays the glory of his riches"—
somehow that goes with the heart's longing. God is at work
among us, leading us by the heart, but we are not there yet,
where we are going.

It is as though the face of the universe were like a human
face that has been sketched out but not completed. Flannery
O'Connor, writing about the face of Mary Ann, a twelve-year-
old girl who had only half a face, the other half being devas-
tated and deformed by a tumor, said "in us the good is
something under construction." The face of Mary Ann, she
said, is the face of the good. It is "grotesque" and yet "full of
promise."[39] That is what I am seeing, I believe, as I hold at
once to the truth of human misery and that of the heart's
longing, the face of a universe that is half-completed, that is
half-deformed and half-beautiful, that is "grotesque" with
human misery and yet "full of promise" with the heart's
desire.

What is happening here is that a vision based on the heart's
longing, that of Teilhard de Chardin in which everything is
converging upon an ultimate point of fulfillment (Omega), is
being modified by a sense of human misery, the sense of the
grotesque in Flannery's stories. For me too, I realize as I
reflect upon this, everything is converging upon Omega, or
really upon Alpha: our journey together in time is toward the
sources of life. For me too there is a face upon the journey that
is half a face, a partial eclipse of the human essence that is
caused by the social relations in which we live. If I live out of
such a vision, if I say "in us the good is something under

construction," I become involved in the construction of the good. I become involved also in a struggle against evil. That construction and that struggle are a matter of our relationship with one another, and my involvement is a matter of my entering into such a relationship, of my joining others on the journey and in the struggle.

A vision of everything converging upon Omega, when you act upon it, means relating to one another in a freedom toward death and the material conditions of life. It means, as Teilhard says in his "syllogism," that

> At the heart of our universe, each soul exists for God, in our Lord. But all reality, even material reality, around each one of us, exists for our souls. Hence, all sensible reality, around each one of us, exists, through our souls, for God in our Lord.[40]

If I bring a sense of human misery to this vision, a sense of the enslavement of human beings to death and material conditions, then moving toward this freedom where everything is for us and we are for God means going on an exodus out of slavery, like the exodus of the Israelites out of Egypt. I see God leading us by the heart's longing on an exodus out of human misery. This exodus, it seems to me, rather than simply resignation to existing conditions as the will of God, is the religion of the poor. It is "the sigh of the oppressed creature" not simply a resignation to being oppressed. It is "the heart of a heartless world" not simply an acquiescence in a world that is heartless. It is "the soul of soulless conditions" not simply a willingness to live in conditions that are soulless. The sigh, the heart, and the soul are the heart's longing, the half face that is beautiful. The oppressed creature, the heartless world, and the soulless conditions are human misery, the half face that is devastated and deformed. The image of God in the religion of the poor is the full face that is yet to be, the "promise" of the half face that now is.

My joining others on the human journey, my joining the

poor in their religion, if I do it consciously and deliberately, becomes a way of working with God, of working toward the image of God. That for me is the meaning of "human practice" (*praxis*), not just human misery working toward its own reversal or the heart's longing working toward its own fulfillment but our working with God leading us by our longing on an exodus out of our misery. My own path in life becomes the road of the exodus for me when I realize where it is coming from and where it is going and how it relates to the paths of others. If I can see all human beings as located at different points on the human circle by their circumstances in life and see the heart's desire as the center of the circle, then I see each human path as a radial path from some point on the circle to the center.[41] What is more, I see all the radial paths converging. The exodus leads from the circumference of human misery to the center of heart's desire. My own path is related to the road of the exodus as a single radial path to the convergence of all paths upon the center. I take the human road by taking my own path, taking it in the awareness that our lives are converging, that the further we go on the paths of heart the closer we come to each other.

Although my own path disappears from view in the convergence of paths upon the center, therefore, I do not actually lose my way. Each radial path from the circumference goes all the way to the center and remains a unique path all the way to the center. There is an insight here, I believe, into the personal journey and personal religion and the particular way. When I first pass over into the journey together and the religion of the poor and the human road, it can seem that I must henceforth leave behind all that is personal. To do so, though, would be "an interior catastrophe," as Teilhard says in a letter at the thought of giving up his personal vision and his personal search for truth. "Obviously I cannot abandon my own personal search," he writes, "—that would involve me in an interior catastrophe and in disloyalty to my most cherished vocation."[42]

An interior catastrophe occurs, it seems, whenever personal knowledge is made to yield to common persuasion. A vision like Teilhard's arising out of the heart's longing or like the one I am coming to by holding at once to the truth of the heart's longing and to that of human misery, though it is a vision of converging paths, is essentially personal knowledge. It is a personal insight into the common experience of the heart's longing and of human misery. "We know more than we can tell," Polanyi says defining personal knowledge, "and we can tell nothing without relying on our awareness of things we may not be able to tell."[43] I can share the vision with others, that is, but I always know more than I am able to share. If I were to abandon the personal grounding of my vision and try to retain only its collective focus, I would actually lose sight of the vision and end by losing my own way in life. I would go backward through Dante's journey, back from his vision of everything converging like a white rose upon its center, back to his starting point where he is lost in a dark wood.

As it is, what I can know of the human road comes of going forward through a kind of divine comedy, passing over into the hell of human misery, the purgatory of naked humanity, and the heaven of heart's desire. All I have to go on in myself when I enter that hell, it is true, are the human needs I have in common with others, and when I enter that purgatory the human essence I share, and when I enter that heaven the universal heart's longing I experience in myself. So there is common ground in the act of passing over, though the act and thus my grounding in the common ground is personal. Bloy has "the woman who was poor" go through fire, a spiritual fire within herself, as her husband goes through physical fire trying to save others in a burning opera house. The flames, as Bloy understands them, are hellfire and the purifying fire of purgatory and ultimately the bright fire of paradise, "that furnace of Beatitude which not even the deluge could quench.''[44] At its best, passing over into the hell of human misery means going through a spiritual fire in myself while others go through physical fire, but passing over into their purgatory means entering a physical fire that is becoming spiritual, and passing over into their heaven means entering into the spiritual fire itself.

Now, as I come back to myself, I can see that this spiritual fire has been a kindling of the heart and an illumining of the mind. I have been going through a "purgative way" and an "illuminative way," as in a mystic's journey, and now I must enter upon a "unitive way" where God's will for us and our own heart's longing are one and the same, where indeed "there is only one misery, and that is—not to be saints." I must let myself become caught up like Dante at the end of his journey in "the love that moves the sun and the other stars." For me, nevertheless, this cannot be the end of the journey, for my divine comedy is only my own entering into our voyage together in time, a journey that is still going on. I have now to ask myself where God is leading us—not to see "past the view" but to see where the road ahead is going before it becomes lost from our sight. *Only God can see the human road through to the end.*

What I am able to do, what I should do, if only God can see the road all the way to the end, if only God can give continued attention and assistance and guidance to the end, is share what I do see of the road, share my vision of "the road past the view." When Black Elk spoke of "a mighty vision" and "a man too weak to use it," he was thinking of the power in his vision of the roads his people had to travel, the red road of good and the black road of troubles and war, and the weakness in his attempt to share his vision with others, the horse dance in which he acted it out with the help of others in symbolic gestures, and then later his attempt to share it by telling the story to a white man. Any attempt I make to share my vision of the human road will have the same weakness. It will be only a symbolic enacting of the vision, a putting of the vision into words. Still, it will carry the power there is in passing over to others and coming back to oneself, the acts that give rise to the vision, and it will make that power available to others. That, in fact, is what it means to act upon the vision, to pass over to others and to come back to oneself.

"But if the vision was true and mighty, as I know, it is true and mighty yet," Black Elk says; "for such things are of the spirit, and it is in the darkness of their eyes that men get lost."[45] There is darkness that can be illumined even by the simple acts of passing over to others and coming back to oneself. It is the darkness that goes before the kindling of spiritual fire, before the kindling of the heart and the illumining of the mind. There is a hint here as to how and where God is leading us. If God leads by kindling our hearts and illumining our minds, then we work with God by passing over to one another and coming back to ourselves. What we are sharing with one another is the spiritual fire. "Take this ring, Master, for your labors will be heavy," Tolkien's sage is told; "but it will support you in the weariness you have taken upon yourself. For this is the Ring of Fire, and with it you may rekindle hearts in a world that grows chill."[46]

What I may hope, if I seek to "rekindle hearts in a world that grows chill" and if God's own work is to kindle hearts and illumine minds, is to reflect what God is doing, to see and say and do what God is doing and thus make it humanly visible. God is at work among human beings, and yet what God is doing may not fully come about unless we see and say and do it. If I can reflect it and make it visible, I may be cooperating with God to bring it to fulfillment. Even a symbolic enactment or a telling in words could be a way of realizing it. Acting it out, telling about it, I am like a boy evoking the sunrise on the first day of summer,[47] seeing and saying and doing what dawn is doing, blowing out street lamps as they go out, blowing out stars as they fade in the growing light, pointing to house after

house as lights go on, giving commands as people wake and
rise and come forth to their daily tasks, conducting the birds
as they sing and fly from the trees, and pointing at last to the
eastern sky as the sun begins to rise.

If the sunrise I am evoking is the kindling of hearts and the
illumining of minds, my seeing and saying and doing it can
have something to do with its actually coming about in human
hearts and minds. I may actually evoke a sense of human
misery and of the heart's longing, an awakening that can lead
someone into passing over to others and coming back to self,
into entering consciously and willingly upon our voyage in
time to eternity. One person's vision can be to another like a
"sun dog" or a "mock sun," as it is also called, or a "weather
gall," a small nearly round halo of light caused by the pres-
ence of ice particles in the atmosphere at dawn. To see the
other person's vision is to see the "sun dog." To see one's own
by passing over to others and coming back to oneself, to feel
the kindling of one's own heart and the illumining of one's
own mind, is to see the sunrise itself. It is to see "fire in the
earth."

"It is done," Teilhard says in his *Mass on the World*. "Once
again the Fire has penetrated the earth . . . the flame has lit
up the whole world from within."[48] That is what I see too if I
look to the heart's longing and see how the heart is kindled
and the mind is illumined. If I look to human misery, how-
ever, especially the misery of the poor, I see "a world that
grows chill." My vision then indeed becomes a "sun dog" or a
"mock sun" or a "weather gall" outlined in light upon ice
particles over the horizon. Or, if I put the two sights together,
the world kindling from within and the world growing chill,
the light and the darkness, it becomes "a lamp shining in a
dark place," as Peter called his vision of Christ transfigured,
"until the day dawns and the morning star rises in your
hearts."[49]

In between the world growing chill and the world kindling

from within comes the point where people are able to differentiate themselves from their lot, the point where the "child of the dark" is able to escape for a while from the *favela*, where "the woman who was poor" is set free for a while from her poverty. It is the turning point, the moment of waiting for the warmth and the light to come. It is the point of no return, for poverty as a way is not the same as misery. As a way it means living by the grace that comes through the void and the fissures of life, through the void of unfulfilled heart's desire and through the fissures of unfulfilled human needs. If God is leading us upon such a way, by the kindling and the illumining that come of living in our naked humanity, then truly he is leading us upon the way taken by Christ, and the vision of Christ transfigured is a vision of our transfigured humanity.

FIVE

God in the Course of Human Events

"Faith in God," the words I saw painted over the doorway of a hut on the Amazon, stand over and against a saying I came upon afterward that the Amazon is "the river that God forgot."[1] Those words, "Faith in God" (*Fé em Deus*), speak of hope and willingness. Those others, "the river that God forgot," speak of oppressed people, of a heartless world, and of soulless conditions.

There is a contrast here that makes me think of an insight I came to once, sitting by a lamp and thinking of the Four Horsemen of the Apocalypse, war and famine and sickness and death.[2] It occurred to me suddenly that what Jesus is doing in the Gospels is just the opposite, peacemaking and feeding the hungry and healing the sick and bringing the dead to life. If what Jesus is doing is what God is doing, I realized, then what God is doing is not the same as what is happening at large in the world. What God is doing is something that is trying to happen, it seemed to me, but does not actually or fully happen unless we live it out in faith. The words, "the river that God forgot," alluding as they do to what was happening on the Amazon during the rubber boom, the exploitation and the inhumanity, suggest something of what is happening in the world at large. The words on the hut, "Faith in God," suggest something of what is going on in the Gospels where the poor and the hungry and the sorrowful and the outcast are the blessed.

"God is vulnerable," a sentence that lives in my memory of a seminar given many years ago by Jacques Maritain,[3] seems to speak to both sides of the insight I am now considering. There is the will of God as it is done "in heaven," and there is the will of God as it is done "on earth." There is what is happening in the Gospels, and there is what is happening or what is failing to happen in the world at large. God is vulnerable in that his will can be thwarted, can fail to be "done on earth as it is in heaven." It is as though human affairs were like a "fail spot" or a "fail place" in a forest, a bare place where forest reproduction has failed. There is a life that is thriving in the forest, but there is a place where the life has not flourished. So too God is at work in the universe, but there is a domain, that of human affairs on earth, where what God is doing depends for its outcome on human freedom and can fail and does fail. Still, things can happen in a clearing, though it is a "fail spot" or a "fail place," that cannot happen in the shadow of the forest. Things can grow there that can grow nowhere else. That seems true also of what God is doing in the course of human events. Things can happen there, as in the Gospels, that are still more marvelous than what happens in the greater universe, though they happen in the midst of failure and barrenness.

Let me see if I can discover God in the course of human events by passing over to the poor and the hungry and the sorrowful and the outcast, by passing over, I say, though I will be talking about myself passing over more than about those I am passing over to, somewhat in the vein of principles (like those of "relativity" and of "uncertainty" in physics) that speak more of the observers of nature than of nature itself. I will speak of myself not as an observer, it is true, but as a participant of human misery and of the heart's longing, but I will be trying to go from God in my consciousness and willingness to God in our knowledge and love.

God in Human Misery

Am I abandoning the religion of the poor when I say, "God is vulnerable" and God's will can fail to be "done on earth as it is in heaven"? On the altiplano in Peru and Bolivia, when some terrible thing happens, people say, "God wills it" (*Dios lo quiere*). There is the assumption that whatever happens is the will of God. Still, "God wills it" is said with sorrow and not with indifference or with despair, and there is not only a willingness to accept what happens as the will of God but also a hope that hidden in the evil, if God is at work, there is something good. *Where is God?* That is the question that arises when you see some terrible thing happen, if you believe there is a God and God is good. It is the question that is posed by every event that seems to go contrary to the goodness of God. If God is indeed at work and there is good hidden in the evil, then the question is more than rhetorical and there is somewhere an answer.

A moment comes in Elie Wiesel's *Night* when a young boy is being hanged in the concentration camp and someone is heard to ask that question "Where is God?" and Wiesel hears a voice within him answer "Where is He? Here He is—He is hanging here on this gallows. . . ."[4] If God is so vulnerable as to suffer in human suffering, then God is there suffering in the poor and the hungry and the sorrowful and the outcast. "I would rather suffer injustice than do it,"[5] Socrates said, and so it seems with God, that God is in those who are suffering injustice rather than in those who are doing it. Yet isn't God at work also in those who are doing it, trying to turn their hearts from evil to good? And what about human suffering when there are no human beings causing it, when it comes about through some natural disaster such as a flood or an earthquake, an event that is called in law an "act of God"? Here, it is true, we do not have that same feeling of present evil that we do when we see the inhumanity of one human being to another. It may be, nevertheless, that God suffers in human suffering here too and that the true act of God here is more like rescue than disaster.

There does exist an image of God suffering in human suffering in the religion of the poor. It is the image of the suffering Christ. Yet one can easily miss the feeling that surrounds the image when one is coming to the religion of the poor from a personal journey in time. It can seem "a symbol of agony and death"⁶ or an image of One who came into the world "with dissatisfaction and a preference for futile sufferings."⁷ That is because on a personal journey one has differentiated oneself even from one's own lot in life, not to speak of the lot of others, and so it seems one stands over and against human suffering, not part of it, free of it, opposed to it. An image of the suffering Christ evokes then a feeling of oppression, for it seems to call one into a suffering that is not one's own, that is needless, that one is unwilling to undergo. It is only when one begins to enter freely into a relationship with one's own life and that of others, when one joins the poor on their journey and embraces human suffering, that the image of Christ begins to seem life giving, to evoke a feeling that we are not alone. Then there appears a connection between suffering and love, between the willingness to undergo suffering and the ability to love.

When I hear or read it said that someone is "incapable of love" ("she reached the conclusion that the son for whom she would have given her life was simply a man incapable of love"),⁸ I am thunderstruck and I ask myself, "Am I capable of love?" What is really at stake when a person is said to be capable or incapable of love, I think now, is a relationship between suffering and will, a willingness or unwillingness to suffer. Let me see if I can come by way of the connection with love to an insight into what God is doing in human suffering.

Consider "the river that God forgot," the Amazon during the days of the rubber boom, the time and the situation in which the Church of the Poor Devil was built. If I may take the time and the situation to be an image of human misery and of the inhumanity of one human being to another, I may take the Church of the Poor Devil itself to be an image of what God is doing. On the one hand there is the boom, the prosperity at Manaus, and on the other there is the inhumanity and the human misery that made it possible—each ton of latex is said to have cost seven lives. The cabaret called "High Life" of Antonio Jose da Costa, the man who called himself "the Poor Devil," was an embodiment of the prosperity. "All night Manaus bars like the High Life dispensed champagne, Scotch, and even caviar—at prices four times higher than in London or New York."[9] Antonio had a signboard (*taboleta*) made, however, showing a ragged fellow (*tipo andrajoso*) with an inscription below reading "The Poor Devil's" (*Ao Pobre Diabo*).[10] It is as though the High Life embodied a prosperity while the sign of the Poor Devil revealed the shadow it cast.

No doubt the meaning of the sign is ironic, Antonio himself is the Poor Devil, and the sign expresses the irony of his own life. Still, the irony of his life reflects that of the time and the situation and really that of the human condition. As Socratic irony is not simply a pretended ignorance, Socrates pretending to be ignorant and willing to learn so he can question others and bring to light their ignorance, but the recognition of a real ignorance underlying the appearance of knowledge, Socrates knowing he really does not know, so here too, I imagine, the irony is not simply a pretense, Antonio pretending to be a poor devil, but the recognition of a real misery underlying the appearance of great prosperity.

As for the irony of his own life, Antonio's sign is said to have been a conversation piece on which he would be asked "Are you the Devil?" and he would answer "No, I am the Poor Devil."[11] A Socratic conversation might begin in a similar way, with Socrates asking, "Am I a monster more complicated and swollen with passion than the serpent Typho, or a creature of a gentler and simpler sort, to whom Nature has given a diviner and lowlier destiny?"[12] The irony for Socrates is in the question, that he is ignorant of what he is; the irony for Antonio is in the answer, that instead of being a devil he is a poor devil. The irony of a life, it seems, can be expressed in either way, as an ignorance concealed beneath knowledge or as an unhappiness concealed beneath happiness. A willingness is needed to recognize it, a willingness to learn, a willingness to suffer. Without the willingness one does indeed seem to encounter a devil, like Ivan Karamazov whose devil, as he says, is "all that's base in me, all that's mean and contemptible."[13] I encounter the devil in me, the one who negates my knowledge, the one who negates my happiness, if I am unwilling to recognize the poor devil in me, the one who is ignorant, the one who is unhappy.

Say I see or think I see in myself "a man incapable of love." If I stop at "incapable," I encounter the devil in me, a spirit of negation who denies me the very possibility of knowledge and love. I may back into a cynical disbelief in human sincerity and benevolence and uprightness and competence, a loneliness that breeds contempt of human beings. If "incapable" can become "capable," on the other hand, if I see the connection between love and suffering and am willing to be the one who is ignorant and unhappy, who has to learn and to go through suffering, I encounter the poor devil in me, a spirit of affirmation who is in touch with the unrealized capacity of my mind and heart. What is more, having found it in myself, I can see the capacity in others, I can see the irony of my times, the ignorance and unhappiness underlying our enlightenment and prosperity, but I can see in our ignorance and unhappiness, realizing it is unrealized, our capacity for knowledge and love. The poor devil in me is wise and happy after all.

It is the connection between my own loneliness and that of others, between my own suffering and that of others, that is the heart of my poor devil's wisdom and happiness. "The simple man knows the essential," Kierkegaard says, "while the wise man little by little learns to know that he knows it, or learns to know that he does not know it."[14] I find "the essential" in suffering and love, in the willingness to learn and to go through suffering and the ability to know and to love. The human condition is there in the learning and suffering we must go through; the human essence is there in our capacity for knowledge and love. If "the simple man knows the essential," it is by way of the religion of the poor. If "the wise man little by little learns to know that he knows" or "that he does not know," it is by way of personal religion. And if "the wise man" learns to know that "the simple man" knows, it is by passing over from personal religion to the religion of the poor. What I learn in passing over is that my own loneliness, the suffering of my own life, is not just a personal affliction, to be dealt with as a personal problem, but is my link to the suffering of humanity.

"He regarded his suffering as a personal affliction for which you might ask a doctor's advice," Jung says of his father; "he did not see it as the suffering of the Christian in general."[15] If I do pass over, if I do regard my suffering as my link to that of humanity, I may see it "as the suffering of the Christian," seeing all human beings linked together in the human circle by their suffering and seeing Christ as the center where all the radial paths meet. "The suffering of the Christian" then is not some particular kind of suffering that others who are not Christians do not undergo but is the suffering of my life when I see it linked to that of others on the path leading from where I am to where Christ is. Deprivation, it is true, is always particular; it is a handicap, a disadvantage, the lack of something that other people seem to have. So it is a source of loneliness, a feeling of being apart from others and wanting to be at one with them.

To be at one with others is to be at the center, at the point of arrival where all the paths meet. To be alone and apart, to feel the element of deprivation in my life, is to be at the point of departure. For it is my particular lack, my handicap combined with everything else in my life, that makes me different and gives me my particular location on the human circle. Even if it is not intimacy with others that I lack, I feel the lack as a kind of loneliness, not having what others have and thus being separated from them. To see the irony of my life, the ignorance underlying my knowledge, the unhappiness underlying my happiness, is to perceive the lack, the poverty in the midst of all the richness I do have. Although it is only one of the many elements in my life, the others being things that belong to my knowledge and my happiness, the element of deprivation qualifies all the others and seems to set them over and against an ignorance and an unhappiness. I am unhappy because I do not have, ignorant because I do not know what it is to have something that I lack. My loneliness is the feeling of the want and the wanting.

Still, I share that very feeling of want and wanting, I share the loneliness with others, and that joins us together in the human circle even before we make our way from the circumference to the center. When I see the link between my own loneliness and that of others, I see how ignorance and unhappiness go deeper than I thought. I see how it is not just a matter of me not knowing what it is to live in dimensions of life that are unfamiliar to me but of us not knowing what it is to live the fullness of human life. We all lack the fullness of life that comes of being whole, of being at the center, and so we are all ignorant of what it is to live human life to the full. All we know of fullness, before we make our way to the center, is our emptiness, our want and our wanting. We know that we do not know, or we know "the essential" in the form of an unrealized capacity for knowing and loving. We know God through emptiness rather than fullness.

"I am poor," God says according to Leon Bloy,[16] and a person becomes one with God by becoming utterly poor in spirit according to Meister Eckhart,[17] wanting and knowing and having nothing other than "I am," like God living in the simplicity of I AM. As it is, I am not willing to live in the poverty of my own existence. My want and my wanting carry me beyond what I now am to what I am becoming on the path to the center. God can be found, nevertheless, in my starting point, in my emptiness. If God can say, "I am poor," deprivation does not separate us from God. We can find God in our unfulfillment by being willing to be poor, not indeed with a will to poverty that would halt the journey toward fullness but with a willingness that can take poverty and deprivation as a starting point. "I think of God as being exactly like me," Zorba says. "Only bigger, stronger, crazier."[18] So it is at each point along the way of the journey. In the end, when "alone" becomes "all one," God to me is a fullness. In the beginning, when "alone" is "alone" and no more, God to me is an emptiness.

I am talking of "God to me," of "God to us," at different points on a journey through suffering to knowledge and love. If I were to suppress the thought of the journey and take God to be simply "God to me" or "God to us" at some given point in time, then I might conclude like Feuerbach that God simply reflects human existence or, if I saw something of the connection with suffering, I might conclude like Marx that God reflects a problem of human existence that has to be solved in purely human terms.[19] If I see, however, that human life cannot be lived to the full without God, that the human essence is a capacity for knowledge and love, that I become able to know and to love by being willing to learn and to go through suffering, then I see how God and suffering cannot be made to vanish.

God is "like me," as Zorba says, "only bigger, stronger, crazier," but that is when I am willing to learn and to go through suffering, when I am able to know and to love. Then I find myself caught up in something that is too big for me, for it encompasses the suffering of all humanity, too strong for me, for it calls for the lover's choice, to give rather than withhold the heart, too crazy for me, for it carries me beyond the limits of my thinking and knowing. "Not I, but God in me,"[20] Hammarskjold says. Only the One who dwells within me, who is "bigger, stronger, crazier," can enable me to embrace the suffering of all humanity, to give my heart, to go beyond the limits of my own mind. "Man does not perceive the truth; God perceives the truth in man."[21] Not I, but God in me knows, loves, endures the truth.

My own part is that of one who "little by little learns to know that he knows" or "learns to know that he does not know" the truth God in me knows. What the truth is comes to light in my human needs, especially in those that are unfulfilled, the element of deprivation in my life, but the whole truth is there in all my needs, fulfilled and unfulfilled, how we need each other for the fullness of human life. "You leave us with our needs," Al-Hallaj says to his God, "not with our sense of glory."[22] There is an almost mystical way on which I am led, first to recognize my own need and seek my own fulfillment, and then on beyond my own fulfillment, "beyond the pleasure principle," to a sense of the whole human circle and the suffering of all humanity. I end up being willing to be in need, if I follow the way, being willing to go through suffering and deprivation rather than simply seek fulfillment, and being able to relate to others out of willingness rather than out of bare need itself. I become capable, that is, of love.

Once I stand in the capability of love I see all that went before in a new light. I see how the real evil was not the element of deprivation in my life but the unwillingness to be in need and to go through suffering, the incapability of love. I see how the dilemma of God and suffering arises out of the feeling that deprivation is the evil, as in the conundrum:

> If God is God He is not good,
> If God is good He is not God. [23]

"If God is God," almighty that is, "He is not good," according to this, does not prevent evil from existing in the world, and "if God is good," wishes to abolish evil but cannot, "He is not God," is not almighty. I see how the insight, on the other hand, comes to light in the capability of love:

> Blow on the coal of the heart
> And we'll see by and by. . . .[24]

It is the incapability of love and the unwillingness that underlies it that gives rise to the inhumanity of one human being to another. The sorrow of God comes ultimately of the clash between the will of God and the unwillingness that makes us incapable of love.

To say God suffers in those who suffer, it is true, or to speak of "the sorrow of God," can seem to say "God is good" in such a way as to deny "God is God." Certainly it seems to run counter to classical theology and the notion that God is above and beyond suffering. Yet it is in accord with the classical notion that sin is "contrary to the fulfillment of the divine will and to the divine love."[25] Actually if we can speak of "God in us" and yet of "God above and beyond us," then we can say "God is good" and yet "God is God." The key is the divine emptiness that is fullness, the thought that "God has no essence," no limiting essence, I mean, that would make God alien to us, and yet no essence that would limit God to us and make God alien to trees or animals or stars. God is at home in us, in our minds and hearts and even in our suffering, if this is true, and yet God is at home also beyond us. The one thing that is alien to God is the unwillingness that makes us incapable of love. The true essence of God, therefore, the essence that is no limiting essence, is revealed in the clash of God with sin in us, in the image of the suffering Christ.

"Jesus will be in agony even to the end of the world,"[26] Pascal says and Rouault writes under an engraving of Jesus on the cross. As long as there is suffering in the world, this seems to say, Christ will suffer in those who suffer. The agony of Christ seems to arise, though, out of the antagonism between willingness and unwillingness, between love and the incapability of love, between humanity and inhumanity. Rouault places this engraving at the beginning of a series on war where he depicts the inhumanity of one human being to another. God is at one with us in our humanity, the image of the suffering Christ seems to say, and in conflict with our inhumanity; it is in that agony and that antagonism that God is vulnerable.

Why does being capable of love depend, therefore, on being willing to go through suffering? It is because loving means going out to the things of life just as knowing means taking them into oneself. When I make the lover's choice, when I give my heart to my life rather than withhold my heart, I enter into a relationship with the things of my life that makes me vulnerable to loss and deprivation. God becomes vulnerable in loving the world, "for God so loved the world. . . . "[27] So if I am unwilling to go through suffering, I become unable to make the lover's choice. If I enter into God's relationship with the world, on the other hand, if I embrace suffering, that of my own life and that of others in its connection with me, I become able to give my heart. I become capable of love and of the knowledge that comes of love. I become capable of God.

God in the Heart's Longing

A lover's choice to be heart and soul in my life is a decision to live to the full capacity of my mind and heart. It is a choice to follow the heart's longing. If the religion of the poor is a cry of the heart, personal religion is a decision to follow the heart.

When I start from personal religion, however, as I have been doing, and pass over to the religion of the poor, I go from choosing to realizing the full dimensions of what I am choosing. For I see human longing expressed in the cry of the heart in its universality where before I knew it only through the particularity of my own life and had difficulty distinguishing it from the dream of having what I do not have. "Hallelujah from the heart of God," sings the insane poet Christopher Smart, expressing in his insanity the true cry of the heart:

> For God the Father Almighty plays upon the harp
> Of stupendous magnitude and melody . . .
> For at that time malignity ceases
> And the devils themselves are at peace . . .
> For this time is perceptible to man
> By a remarkable stillness and serenity of soul. [28]

Although the cry uttered in the religion of the poor is a cry for deliverance, it is nevertheless a cry of heart and soul, a "hallelujah from the heart of God" that is "perceptible to man by a remarkable stillness and serenity of soul." It gives expression to the capacity of our mind and heart and not just to our dream of having what we do not have. There is deliverance, "for at that time malignity ceases," human beings desist from their inhumanity to one another, "and the devils themselves are at peace," the dark forces at work in the human heart, the demons an insane person knows in his insanity, are at rest. Yet the deliverance comes from deep within the heart where God is dwelling. The cry is of the human heart and soul, and yet it is a "hallelujah from the heart of God" as if the harp on which God is playing were strung with human heartstrings. It is a cry to God for deliverance, and yet it is God's own cry to God, and so it contains in itself the very deliverance it invokes, felt in "a remarkable stillness and serenity of soul," a peace of heart and soul, a heart's longing that becomes, when it is expressed, an heartsease.

Our capacity of mind and heart is hard to tell from our dream of having what we do not have. For the capacity is unrealized and the dream is unfulfilled. The difference comes out, though, in the expression. "All sorrows can be borne," Isak Dinesen says, "if you put them into a story or tell a story about them."[29] If I tell my story of not having, the story of my loneliness, I am giving expression also to my dream of having, but I am not bringing my dream to fulfillment. I am still alone. My sorrow at not having, nevertheless, my loneliness can be borne if I put it into a story or tell a story about it, if I sing of it like Christopher Smart singing his song of madness. For in the telling or the singing my capacity of mind and heart is being realized. Expression is not a fulfillment of my dream, but it is a realization of my capacity. "Within our whole universe the story only has authority to answer that cry of heart of its characters," Dinesen says, "that one cry of heart of each of them: *Who am I?*"[30]

Expression speaks to the heart of personal religion, to the cry, "Who am I?"; it speaks also to the heart of the religion of the poor, to "the sigh of the oppressed, the heart of a heartless world, and the soul of soulless conditions." It speaks to the heart because it speaks from the heart, even from "the heart of God." Only that mad "hallelujah from the heart of God" can answer the human heart, it seems, can bring the moment of "stillness and serenity," the moment when "malignity ceases." Let me see if I can discover "the heart of God" in the personal "cry of heart" and in the sigh, the heart and the soul of the poor.

How does the cry for identity "Who am I?" relate to the cry for deliverance of the poor, let me ask, and how can the mere expression, the utterance of the cry, bring heartsease? There may be a clue in the story of the Poor Devil. Just as Antonio had a signboard in his cabaret reading "The Poor Devil's" (*Ao Pobre Diabo*), so too Cordolina, the woman who lived with him and built the chapel that came to be known as the Church of the Poor Devil, opened a bar and called it "The Poor Devil's" but in the feminine gender (*A Pobre Diaba*).[31] The name is an answer, both for the man and the woman, to the question, "Who am I?" It is also an expression, however ironic, of the cry for deliverance, meaning as it does "a person in misery." With all its irony the name passed from the man and the woman, from the cabaret and the bar, to the chapel and to the largo where the chapel was located and to the streetcar that went to the largo, and ended, with the disappearance of all the rest, as the name of the chapel alone. It is as though the name passed from personal irony to the very truth of the poor and their religion.

I am moving in the same direction, from the cry for identity to the cry for deliverance. When I ask, "Who am I?" and look to the story of my life for an answer, I come upon a truth I can hardly endure. As I try to make the lover's choice and give my heart to my life I see in retrospect that I have not loved, that I have lived out of my unfulfilled human needs, that I have related to others out of emptiness rather than fullness. I can be crushed by my self-knowledge if there is no greater truth, no whole truth encompassing the truth I now know. I see the point of Augustine's cry, when instead of asking only, "Who am I?" he prays "that I may know me, that I may know thee."[32] For if I ask to know myself, to know God, I am asking not only for the truth but for the whole truth, and my cry for identity anticipates the cry for deliverance. I am ready to join the lame, the halt and the blind crying out to be made whole.

If I were to call myself "the Poor Devil," like Antonio and Cordolina, I would be thinking of being lonely and loveless, but I would be passing from irony to humor. There is wit in the name being used for a cabaret and a bar, but there is humor in its passing to a chapel, a largo, and a streetcar. There is wit in Antonio calling himself by that name with the signboard in his cabaret. There is wit in Cordolina calling herself that too, opening her bar, but there is humor in her having a little statue of Santo Antonio in her bar (the bar is gone but the statue still exists)[33] and in her building a chapel for Santo Antonio that came to be called the Church of the Poor Devil. "The ironist levels everything on the basis of humanity in the abstract," Kierkegaard says, "the humorist on the abstract God-relationship,"[34] as if the ironist were saying everyone is a poor devil and the humorist everyone is a poor devil before God, "abstract" for the humorist "does not enter concretely into this relationship, but it is just at this point that he parries by means of the jest." If one does enter concretely into the God-relationship, as Cordolina does and I want to do, then one drops the mask of humor or, as Kierkegaard has it, steps out of the "incognito" of humor. One joins those who are truly poor devils, the poor, the hungry, the sorrowful, the outcast, the blessed of the Gospel.

Before I drop the mask or step out of the incognito, I learn something about being a poor devil. It is that the ironist is right, everyone is a poor devil, and the humorist is right, everyone is a poor devil before God. "What the simple religious man does directly," Kierkegaard says, "the simple man of knowledge does only through humor."[35] That corresponds to what he says about the simple man knowing "the essential" and the simple wise man learning "to know that he knows" or "to know that he does not know." When I learn that I have been living out of my needs, out of my emptiness, I learn that I am a poor devil, that I have these unfulfilled needs, and that I am a poor devil before God, that I have been living out of emptiness rather than fullness. I learn at the same time, though, that we are all poor devils, that we all have these needs, and that we are all poor devils before God, that we all live out of our emptiness in relating to one another. I learn to know that I know the lovelessness, or to know that I do not know the love except through the void of love.

After I drop the mask and step out of the incognito of being a poor devil, however, I learn something more. It is that true humanity, as distinct from "humanity in the abstract," and the true relationship with God, as distinct from "the abstract God-relationship," is to be found with the blessed of the Gospel, with those who are poor and hungry and sorrowful and outcast. I find too that I am not excluded, that no one is excluded from their number. All the irony of everyone being a poor devil, and all the humor of everyone being a poor devil before God, gets swallowed up in joining them. For what makes them blessed is not their deprivation itself but the heart's longing felt in the depths of their deprivation, and what enables me to join them is my own feeling of those depths and that longing. It is there in the depths and the longing of the human heart that I am able to hear the "hallelujah from the heart of God."

There is the "darkness of the human heart," to be sure, "the basic unreliability of men who never can guarantee today who they will be tomorrow."[36] At first all I can hear in the darkness is the cry of my own heart, "Who am I?" It is when I find I am unable to guarantee today who I will be tomorrow, having still to realize the lover's choice, to be heart and soul in the relationships of my life, that it becomes a cry for deliverance, and it is when I join the others who are crying for deliverance, the poor, the hungry, the sorrowful, the outcast, that it becomes the divine cry in the human heart. For then it is love coming through the void of love, enabling me to love. It tells me who I am and who the others are. The poor become "the poor in spirit," the hungry become "those who hunger and thirst for righteousness," the sorrowful become "those who mourn" with the sorrow of God, and the outcast become "those who are persecuted for righteousness' sake."[37]

Who then am I? I am the voice of my own heart's cry as it goes through its changes, from the cry for identity to the cry for deliverance to the divine cry in the human heart. I am the voice of the cry, the expression of it, that is, and so I find heartsease in expression itself. Character, according to Yeats, is "the Will analysed in relation to the enforced Mask"; personality is "the Will analysed in relation to the free Mask"; and individuality is "the Will analysed in relation to itself."[38] As I go from the cry for identity to the cry for deliverance, trying and discarding the masks of irony and humor, and on to the divine cry in my heart, I seem to go from enforced and free expression to something that has no proper expression other than itself. I come to my naked individuality, according to Yeats' formula "the Will analysed in relation to itself," according to Kierkegaard's formula the self "relating itself to its own self" and "willing to be itself" and "grounded transparently" in God.[39] I go through a kind of stripping of enforced and free masks and am reduced to my bare will, a will that becomes a willingness to follow God in my heart.

Who then are the poor, the hungry, the sorrowful, the outcast? They are those who live in their naked humanity, and the blessed are those who know God in their naked humanity. I can see in the religion of the poor that there is a knowing of God among those who have nothing but their own bodies, their own hearts, their own minds and God. I begin to understand it when I come to my own naked individuality, when I am reduced to the poverty of my own existence. For then I ask, "Why do I exist?" and "Why is there anything at all and not rather nothing?"[40] If I receive my own existence as a gift, I become "grounded transparently" in God. I revert, as it were, to preexistence in the mind of God where, as Meister Eckhart says, "what I wanted, I was and what I was, I wanted."[41] I become willing at last, after so long being unwilling, to live in the poverty of my own existence. When I receive my own existence as a gift, though, reduced as I am to my naked individuality, I can see how the poor, the hungry, the sorrowful, the outcast know God in their naked humanity. They too receive their existence as a gift, and I am standing with them in their relationship with God.

To receive our existence as a gift, nevertheless, does not

mean taking our condition in life as a gift. "It is not *how* the world is, that is the mystical," Wittgenstein says, "but *that* it is."[42] So too it is not *how* we are, our having and our not having, but *that* we are, that is mystical, that is blessed, that is gift. Living in our naked humanity, living in my naked individuality, is a matter of relationship, the will relating to itself and becoming the willingness to exist, to receive life, to be grounded in God. It is like looking up into the night sky and feeling the wonder, letting what is most taken for granted, the existence of things, become a wonder, ceasing even to take my own existence for granted and letting it too become a wonder. At that moment of wonder at existence and my own existence I perceive the divine cry:

> Hallelujah from the heart of God,
> And from the hand of the artist inimitable,
> And from the echo of the heavenly harp
> In sweetness magnifical and mighty. [43]

It is a cry that is "from the heart of God." For if the world is, then the world is loved, and if I am, then I am loved. I perceive the love, though, only when existence becomes a wonder for me. Then I discern "the hand of the artist inimitable"; then I hear "the echo of the heavenly harp in sweetness magnifical and mighty." As long as I am caught up in how the world is, in how I am, taking for granted that it is and that I am, I cannot make out the divine cry. I am busy relating things to other things in a world and a life that is given. It is only when I relate the world to itself and me to myself, realizing it is given and I am given, that I begin to wonder at existence. It is then that I hear the divine "hallelujah," the cry of God in the story of creation, "and God saw that it was good" and that "it was very good."[44]

Self-relation is the key, "the Will analysed in relation to itself," relating me to myself, relating even the world to itself. It is the key not only in personal religion, I believe, but also in the religion of the poor. Self-relation in personal religion means living in your naked individuality, like Kierkegaard wanting to have inscribed on his tombstone the words "That Individual."[45] By relating myself to my own self, according to his formula, and willing to be myself, I am "grounded transparently" in God. By wondering at my own existence, in other words, and embracing my own existence, I am consciously and willingly receiving my existence as a gift. There is a stripping and a nakedness in this, as I go from living in my character and personality, relating to what I must be and to what I want to be, to living in my individuality, relating to the simple fact that I am. My path in life is shaped by those two factors: character (will in relation to what I must be) determines my starting point, and personality (will in relation to what I want to be) determines my goal. When I let go of them to live out of my individuality (will in relation to itself), my path seems to vanish and I am left with nothing but myself. The secret of individuality, however, is that will relating to itself becomes willingness, becomes consent, becomes Yes. The path I devise for myself vanishes but the path meant for me opens before me.

Something similar happens in the religion of the poor where self-relation means living in your naked humanity. Consider again the woman of the *favela*. She lives at first out of something corresponding to character, will in relation to what we must be, calling her first diary "Garbage Dump" (*Quarto de Despejo*). The *favela* is the garbage dump where she must live, and her diary is the story of her relation to an enforced condition of life. Then, when she escapes from the *favela*, she comes to something corresponding to personality, will in relation to what we want to be, calling the continuation of her diary "Brick House" (*Casa de Alvenaria*).[46] Her new situation is the brick house where she had always dreamed of living, and her diary is the story of her relation to a condition of life that is sought-for and thus "free." Then finally, disillusioned and impoverished once more, she comes to something corresponding to individuality, will in relation to itself, saying, "One can live better when one is poor than when one is rich" and "perhaps that is why Jesus Christ chose to be poor."[47] Her life from this point to her death is poverty enforced and yet free, and seems to be the story of her living in her naked humanity. A life opens before her that is conscious and willing.

As I pass over from my own consciousness and willingness to hers, I go over from a willingness to be myself to a realization of what it is to be myself, what it is really to be a human being. If my naked individuality consists of will in relation to itself, our naked humanity consists of a capacity for knowledge and love. The link between the two appears in the lover's choice. That choice to be heart and soul in my life is the willingness of will in relation to itself. It is the Yes to our capacity for knowledge and love. As long as I remain in myself without passing over, I see the Yes simply as a willingness to be myself, and I see myself as that very will in relation to itself—where there is will there is self, and where there is no will there is no self. When I pass over, though, I find in our shared humanity what it is I am saying Yes to, the capacity for God, the infinity of mind and heart.

"Soul is capable of God,"[48] Aquinas says. It is an inexhaustible capacity for knowledge and for love. That is what I come to realize, passing over from my own stance between enforced and free masks to that of poor people like the woman of the *favela* standing between enforced and free conditions of life. The enforced mask of character and the free mask of personality, when they are stripped away, leave me relating myself to my own self, finding selfhood in my will and my willingness. An enforced condition of life and a free condition, when you are extricated and differentiated from them, leave you relating the world to itself, finding humanity in your sheer existence knowingly and lovingly received as a gift from God.

As I pass over then from selfhood to humanity, from who I am to what I am, consciousness deepens into knowledge and willingness into love. I go from a consciousness of being conscious and a willingness to be willing, from a mind and a heart that circle back upon themselves, to a knowledge and a love that reach through my own longing to know and to love, that reach through and beyond to the very "heart of God."

It is true, knowledge and love have at first to do with the things of life rather than with God, knowledge taking the things in and love going out to the things. When I come to knowledge and love with a consciousness and a willingness that circle back upon themselves, however, as I am doing, my knowledge and my love circle back upon the longing to know and to love and, if I don't halt at the longing itself, carry me on toward the knowledge and love that are the heart of the universe. Consciousness deepens into knowledge, therefore, as I pass over, but knowledge circles back upon itself toward the divine "knowing of knowing." Willingness deepens into love, but love circles back upon itself toward "the love that moves the sun and the other stars."[49] I am already "grounded transparently" in God by my consciousness and my willingness, but God becomes, as I pass over into knowledge and love, my focus as well as my ground.

"The more the wise man thinks about the simple, the more difficult it becomes for him," Kierkegaard says. "And yet he feels himself gripped by a profound humanity, which reconciles him with the whole of life."[50] That is what is happening to me, I can see, as I pass over from personal religion to the religion of the poor. "The wise man" here is the person of consciousness and willingness; "the simple man" is the person of knowledge and love; and "the simple" is what knowledge and love are about. The more I think about knowledge and love, with all my consciousness and my willingness, the more difficult they become for me. And yet I do feel myself gripped by a profound humanity, which reconciles me with the whole of life. It is the humanity of the poor, the hungry, the sorrowful, the outcast. It reconciles me with the whole of life because it leads me to understand the heart's longing, to understand what it is to know and to love.

God's Eyes and Heart

What is it then to know? What is it to love? Thinking about "the simple," I have come upon a connection between love and suffering, between the ability to love and the willingness to suffer, and now upon a cry of heart that gives expression to our capacity for knowledge and love, the cry that comes "from the heart of God." It is willingness to suffer that enables us to love, I have found in thinking about the inability to love, and it is willingness that actually becomes love, I find in passing over to those who know and love, as consciousness becomes knowledge. Willingness then, the will in relation to itself, and the consciousness that goes with it, self-consciousness, is my way into the way of knowledge and love, "of knowing and being known in our naked humanity." Willingness as I have reflected on it here has taken many shapes: to walk alone, to be in need of other human beings, to go through suffering, to be oneself. In all of these forms, let me propose now, it is one and the same thing. If there is a significant change, it is the change that occurs as willingness deepens into love, as will goes out to the things of life before coming back to itself.

This is the heart of passing over, this going out to the things of life, and of coming back, this coming back of will to itself. There is a welcome to the things, a welcome of knowledge and love. "Love bade me welcome," George Herbert says in a poem called "Love,"[51] "yet my soul drew back, guilty of dust and sin." I feel the welcome as I pass over, entering into the religion of the poor, yet I draw back conscious of guilt and mortality. I want to come back to myself before I have really passed over, for I am at home with my guilt and my mortality, with "I am" and "I will die," with the realm of personal religion. "But quick-eyed Love, observing me grow slack from my first entrance in," Herbert says, "drew nearer to me, sweetly questioning, if I lacked anything." The welcome is to a sharing of life. I felt it when people welcomed me to the novena and to the blessing of the bread and to the procession at the Church of the Poor Devil. Do I lack anything?

"A guest worthy to be here." That is Herbert's answer to Love. It is mine to the poor. I am not worthy to be here, to enter into the religion of the poor, for I am not one of the poor, the hungry, the sorrowful, the outcast. "You shall be he." That is Love's reply. It is also that of the poor. I shall be one of them, one of the blessed of the Gospel. "I, the unkind, ungrateful? Ah, my dear, I cannot look on thee," Herbert says. Nor can I look on the poor without feeling my guilt and my mortality. "Love took my hand," says Herbert, "and smiling did reply, 'Who made the eyes but I?' " The poor take my hand too, and give me eyes to see human misery, to see the heart's longing. "Truth, Lord, but I have marred them"; Herbert says of his eyes, "let my shame go where it doth deserve." I have marred mine too, averting them from the sight of human misery and thus missing the depth also of the heart's longing. "And know you not who bore the blame?" says Love, now revealed as Christ. So the poor can say to me. Am I to shoulder the burden of guilt and hold aloof, or am I to let Christ shoulder it and become myself free among the poor?

"My dear then I will serve," Herbert answers, offering to serve Christ. And I will serve the poor, I resolve. "You must sit down and taste my meat," Christ says. So too the poor will not allow a friend to serve but only to join them and share their life. "So I did sit and eat," Herbert says. And so I did join the poor in the novena and in the blessing of bread and in the procession. Is that what it is to know and to love?

It is to see with God's eyes, I will say, and to feel with God's heart. "My eyes and my heart will be there for all time,"[52] God says of the Temple. I would have God say it also of the

Church of the Poor Devil. If what is happening there can be taken as an image of what God is doing, then God is doing what Love is doing in Herbert's poem, inviting us into a sharing of life. On the morning of the festival of Santo Antonio there was the blessing of bread, small buns distributed among as many people as came. I came late, but the *zeladora*, the woman who took care of the chapel, filled a whole sack for me with bread that was leftover. Not being able to eat it all myself, I brought it along with me when I returned there in the evening. The people waiting then for the procession to start, when I opened the sack and showed them the bread, saw without any word from me that it was blessed bread and reached into the sack and helped themselves to it. Soon my sack was empty, and I was glad. I had part in the sharing, it seemed to me, in the giving as well as the receiving.

A sharing of life, if that is what knowledge and love are about, means I am able to love if I am able to share, able to give and to receive. It means our capacity for knowledge and love is a capacity for sharing, for receiving the things of life into ourselves and giving ourselves to the things of our life. A sharing of divine life, as in the poem "Love," means letting Love give me eyes ("who made the eyes but I?") and letting Love carry the burden of my inability to love ("and know you not who bore the blame?") and so sitting down to eat, to share in divine knowledge and love, to see with God's eyes and feel with God's heart. It is knowing and loving God but by knowing what God knows and loving what God loves, the persons and situations of life, letting God be the inner focus, the knower and the lover. And so sharing life with one another can mean sharing divine life—sharing a bread that is blessed.

Now a love feast, a sharing of blessed bread, seems to be only a token. Yet it is actually closer than that to the reality of a sharing of life. For the reality is a matter not simply of the things of life but of a relationship to the things. The real sharing is in the knowing and the loving. No doubt, the love feast can be an empty show if the knowing and the loving are not there, and there are many other ways of giving expression to knowledge and love besides the sharing of blessed bread. If I enter into the love feast with all my mind and all my heart, nevertheless, I do find myself entering into a real sharing of life. I am passing over, as I was doing on the riverboat, from the indefinite longing of my own heart, or even from a longing that arises out of human ties like that of the people from the cabins, to an actual sharing of life like that of the people from the hammocks. So I feel all the hesitancy that Herbert feels, invited to a love feast by Love. I feel how far removed I am from any real sharing of life, living as I do in my longing. I seem to be living not in knowledge and love but in a longing to know and to love.

There is a circuit or a circulation of knowledge and love, "a circle in the acts of the soul,"[53] Aquinas says, starting with the things of life and going from there to the mind, as we take things in by knowing them, and from there to the heart, as knowing leads into loving, and from there back to the things of life, as we go out to things by loving them. Then the circle goes round again, as the loving leads into new knowing and the knowing into new loving. When I enter into a sharing of life with others, I am entering into this round dance of mind and heart, letting others have a mind and heart-changing effect upon me. Living in my heart's longing, however, has led to an inwardness that will not allow me to be entirely at the mercy of the persons and situations of my life, even when I do let them have their effect. When I come to know and to love, I do so always in terms of my longing to know and to love. I wonder then if my longing is enough, if I have the eyes, if I have the heart.

It is by way of longing, as it turns out, that consciousness becomes knowledge and willingness becomes love. "You are a man of desires," the prophet Daniel is told, and in another version, "You are greatly beloved."[54] As I enter into the sharing of life I find myself going from being "a man of desires" to being "greatly beloved." I find my longing to know becoming knowledge and my longing to love becoming love. "Now contemplation and desire, united into one," as Yeats says, "inhabit a world where every beloved image has bodily form, and every bodily form is loved."[55] This is what I call *heartsease*. It is as though the round dance of mind and heart were so swift as to look still from very swiftness. There is stillness, and yet there is movement. It is like "The Round Dance" (*La Ronde*)[56] by Picasso where stick figures of all the races of the world, brown and white and red and yellow, are shown dancing around a dove of peace. So too I am sharing life with others, with all the peoples of the world, and our sharing is a knowing and a loving, and though I bring to it only a longing to know and to love I am caught up in the knowing and the loving and I find knowledge and love myself to my heart's content.

A love feast, a circle of knowledge and love, an heartsease— that sounds like the kingdom of God. It is the blessedness of the poor, the hungry, the sorrowful, the outcast, "for theirs is the kingdom of heaven . . . for they shall be comforted . . . for they shall inherit the earth . . . for they shall be filled. . . . " I seem far from the kingdom as I begin in the solitude of my own heart, but near when I pass over into a sharing of life and discover in my own longing to know and to love my feeling of the human capacity for knowledge and love. Here are the eyes and the heart I have been seeking. If "soul is capable of God," as Aquinas says, it is because "soul is somehow all,"[57] able to take in all by knowledge, able to go out to all by love. It is because "there is no history but that of the soul," as Hammarskjold says, "no peace but that of the soul."[58] Here in the history of the soul, in the peace of the soul, in the "all" of knowledge and love, I find the kingdom of God.

Our capacity for knowledge, I begin to realize as I enter into the sharing of life with others, is our ability to participate in the reality of the things we know. It is "a participation of ours in the existence of that which we comprehend."[59] Participation, when it is felt, is felt as compassion. I cannot know without compassion, if I pursue knowledge as I have been doing, by passing over to others and coming back to myself. All I learn in sharing life with others seems to come by way of compassion, of entering into the suffering of others, of entering into their heart's longing and their heartsease. For there is in compassion a feeling for the suffering of another along with a desire for its alleviation. So there is really a feeling for all three elements: suffering and desire or heart's longing and alleviation or heartsease. What happens in compassion is that my capacity for suffering enables me to enter into the suffering of another, even though it is not my own suffering, and come to the insight it brings. Knowledge so understood extends as far as the sharing of life, as far as soul, and if we can say, "Soul is somehow all," then it extends to all things and all knowledge. The eyes I acquire by passing over and coming back are eyes of compassion like those terrible eyes of God that Nietzsche could not bear, those eyes that "saw you through and through."[60]

Those eyes are terrible when they are separated from "the heart of God," when they seem eyes of pity, as they did to Nietzsche, rather than of compassion. If there is a difference between pity and compassion, it is between a feeling that comes of observing the suffering of another and one that comes of participating in the suffering of another. I feel "those terrible eyes" when I feel myself the object of divine pity. When those eyes become my eyes, on the other hand, I feel myself the companion of God, sharing in God's suffering and God in mine. It is compassion, accordingly, rather than pity that I find in "the heart of God." Love is compassion, going out to those who suffer, or if there is a difference it is between simply suffering with another and being willing to go through suffering with another. Love is the willingness or again, if there is a difference, it is the willingness when it deepens into the choice of being heart and soul with the persons and in the situations of life. (I heard Paul Tillich say once that the difference between love and compassion is that love contains an element of judgment—I would say an element of choice.)[61] The heart I acquire by making the lover's choice, by making myself vulnerable to all the loss that can come to me through the persons and the situations of my life, is "the heart of God." God's heart becomes my heart. I become vulnerable as "God is vulnerable."

We come to know and to love, I am saying, by way of participation in the reality of the things we know and love, and we come, when participation is conscious and willing, to see with God's eyes and feel with God's heart. It is participation that is expressed in a love feast, that is enacted in a sharing of life, that is realized in heartsease. If I ask myself the hard questions that Plato asks himself about participation, I come upon an insight here. Shall we say things "do not mingle, and are incapable of participating in one another?" he asks. "Or shall we gather all into one class of things communicable with one another? Or are some things communicable and others not?"[62] Plato is talking about archetypes, about Being, Motion, Rest, the Same and the Other. I can ask those questions, nevertheless, about the human being, about human suffering and the heart's longing, the repose of mind and heart, the self and the other person.

Before I pass over, it does indeed seem that things "do not mingle, and are incapable of participating in one another." I live in the solitude of my own heart and from there I look out on the suffering of others with eyes of pity but not yet of compassion. I feel "pity and terror" as at a tragic drama, pity for others and fear for myself at the sight of their fate, and I may go through a kind of "catharsis"[63] or purification of those feelings, passing through the pity and the terror to a calmness of mind and heart, but I stand all the while, as it seems to me, outside of all the suffering. My fear for myself, the "terror" in the "pity and terror," prevents me from entering into the suffering any more than I have to, and my desire for the alleviation of suffering remains only a wish, as having nothing to do with myself. My feeling for alleviation or heartsease is simply the relief I feel from emerging out of my own pity and fear, the calmness I attain. I cannot really understand the misery of the poor, I see, nor their religion and heart's longing nor their joy and heartsease as long as I stand outside.

I begin to pass over as soon as I realize that I am not really outside as I thought, that I have been inside the human circle all along, that we do participate in the reality of one another's existence. Now I begin to think we should "gather all into one class of things communicable with one another." My pity at the sight of others suffering, as I become conscious of being one with them, begins to change into compassion. My terror changes too, my fear for myself, as I realize that I do not stand apart from them—it is as though what I fear has already occurred. Instead of a catharsis of pity and terror now I go through a purification of my heart's longing, as my longing to know and to love becomes knowledge and love, as longing changes from the cry for identity "Who am I?" that comes from the solitude of my own heart to a cry for deliverance that comes from a sense of participating in the existence of others to a divine cry, a "hallelujah" that comes of knowing with God's mind and loving with God's heart. Still, I do not find heartsease with others, and the divine cry leads me back into myself, back into the grounding of my knowing and loving, back to its inner focus in the God who knows and loves within me.

After I come back to myself, it seems after all that "some things" are "communicable and others not." That is the position Plato comes to in the end, reflecting on the archetypes. I come to it after seeing what it is to enter into the lives of others and then return to my own life. What is incommunicable, it seems, is being myself. Although I pass over into the suffering and the heart's longing and even the heartsease of others, I cannot rest there. I must come back to my own suffering and my own longing. It is only there that I find my own heartsease. There is not a single thing we do not have in common, even selfhood. I can enter into the selfhood of others, "the Will analysed in relation to itself," and others can enter into mine. Yet I must return to my own self and they to their own selves. The archetype Plato is interested in here is that of the Other, for that to his mind is the archetype of nonbeing. The archetype I am coming upon is that of the Same or its human counterpart, that of the Self. It is the starting point and the ending point of this whole process of passing over and coming back. Yet the Other is what the process is about, what I am passing over to and coming back from. Does the connection with nonbeing mean that in all my passing over I have never really left myself?

Here is the insight I come to, asking all these questions about participation. It is that I do not really go outside of myself to find others. Just as I am not really outside of them, as I thought before passing over, so also they are not really outside of me, as I see now after coming back to myself. I find God in the solitude of my own heart. Yet I find God there only when my participation in the existence of others has become conscious and willing. If I try to answer now the question I started with, "Where is God?" I must say, *God is there in all we know and love but in the knowing and the loving.* We participate in the reality of all we know and love, that is, but we find God there when participation is conscious and willing, when we are seeing with God's eyes and feeling with God's heart.

"Who made the eyes but I?" Love's question in Herbert's poem, seems to imply that seeing with God's eyes means simply seeing with our own eyes and, since it is Love who asks, feeling with God's heart means simply feeling with our own heart. Or vice versa, and this says more, seeing and feeling with our own means seeing and feeling with God's. I was seeing with my own eyes and feeling with my own heart, as I thought, when I was traveling on the riverboat or visiting the Church of the Poor Devil or taking part in the festival. Yet I am seeing with God's eyes and feeling with God's heart now, as I hope, when I am coming back to myself and coming to realize what I have been doing. Seeing with God's eyes, if this is it, is not seeing something other than you see with your own, but realizing or recognizing what you are seeing, realizing your connection, recognizing your kinship with what you are seeing, saying (as God says in Scripture), "I know you." Feeling with God's heart, if Love gives us the eyes, is not feeling something other than you feel with your own, but being willing to feel what you are feeling, being willing to have the connection or the kinship, saying (again as God says in Scripture), "I am with you."[64]

"And know you not who bore the blame?" Love's further question, bears upon the connection, the kinship we have with all we know and love. Our unwillingness to go through suffering, our incapability of love is a severing of the connection, a withdrawal from the kinship, and our responsibility for being unwilling and incapable is "the blame." Love is able to be the one "who bore the blame" because responsibility is itself a connection in the disconnectedness, a relation in the unrelatedness. So Love is able by bearing the responsibility to restore the connection, to reestablish the relation. Our participation in the reality of all we know and love is broken thus and mended. It is like knowing a language, then forgetting it, and then learning it again: the learning is a remembering, a going backward through the process of forgetting. Love bearing "the blame" is Love starting with us where we are in our forgetfulness and leading us to memory. Love being Love, embodying "I know you" and "I am with you," can be with us even where we are in our separation and yet bring us to where we know and are with one another in the participation of humanity.

Once as I sat thinking of the Four Horsemen of the

Apocalypse, war and famine and sickness and death, and of Jesus in the Gospels, making peace and feeding the hungry and healing the sick and raising the dead, I came to an insight setting God over and against the banes of human existence. Now as I reflect on the Church of the Poor Devil, passing over to the poor and the hungry and the sorrowful and the outcast, I come to a further insight. If compassion is a feeling for the suffering of another along with a desire for its alleviation, then God is in the suffering as well as in the desire and in the alleviation. God is there in the knowing and the loving, in the eyes and heart of compassion, in the knowing that comes from suffering, in the loving that is in the heart's longing, in the circle of knowing and loving that is around heartsease. God is there, as in Christ suffering and glorified, in the power of knowledge and love.

SIX

The Happy Ending
of Time

As I reflect on human misery and the heart's longing, I think
of Marx looking forward to an ending of historical conflict in a
classless society. I think also of Freud trying to speak to time
and consciousness out of the timelessness of the unconscious.[1]
I seem again to be passing from irony to humor, it is true, if I
try to envisage the New Jerusalem as a Church of the Poor
Devil. It is possible, nevertheless, to find in the very vision
itself of human misery and the heart's longing a moment of
peace in the midst of conflict, a moment of timelessness out of
which we can speak to time, a moment like that in the title
scene of Tolstoy's *War and Peace* where Prince Andre is lying
wounded on the battlefield and looking up into the infinite
sky, seeing and feeling peace in the midst of war. "How quiet,
peaceful and solemn; not at all as I ran," he says to himself,
"not as we ran, shouting and fighting. . . . "[2]

It is like a moment of peace in a life of restless searching, when you cease to be unhappy for a while by being with people who are simple and carefree in their goodness, when you cease to be uneasy with yourself by being with people who are at one with themselves. You treasure such a moment, carry it with you carefully ever after, let it become a sign of hope, a sign that the peace you are seeking really exists:

> I shall remember this moment. The silence, the twilight, the bowls of strawberries and milk, your faces in the evening light. Mikael sleeping, Jof with his lyre. I'll try to remember what we have talked about. I'll carry this memory between my hands as carefully as if it were a bowl filled to the brim with fresh milk. And it will be an adequate sign—it will be enough for me.[3]

An Omega comes to light in such a moment, a happy ending, a consummation of human affairs. We seem able to see for a moment where everything is leading, what everything is about, why everything is happening. Something good is trying to happen, we see, but it does not succeed in happening unless we do see it, unless we become aware of it. To see it is like passing into the eye of a hurricane where all is still, where there is, as sometimes at the center of a tropical cyclone, a sunlit clear sky. The hurricane in human affairs, a restless pursuit of purpose, a restless conflict of purpose and cross-purpose, arises when human beings become unwilling to go on living out their fate without question. A vision occurs when you encounter the storm, a vision of the world as a continual conflict. But the vision changes in a moment of peace. A transformation of human fate is seen, a transformation that allows human beings to be at one with themselves and with one another. Imagine coming to such a vision. Imagine encountering the hurricane and then passing into the eye.

I came to such a vision, it seemed, when I saw the richness of life on our riverboat voyage up the Amazon, when I saw the stillness and emptiness of the chapel of the Poor Devil, when I saw the light shining in the darkness at the festival. I found a moment of peace, of timelessness, in passing over to the people on the riverboat and to those at the chapel and to those in the festival, but I see in coming back to myself how I have to keep moving, to keep passing over and coming back, to stay in the eye, to follow the path of the hurricane. I see eternity as a vertical and time as a horizontal dimension. I see eternity passing through time, moving as we move in time.

There is an at-onement with others in passing over, I found on the riverboat in passing over to the people from the hammocks and the people from the cabins, and there is an at-onement with oneself in coming back, I found in coming back from them to myself. And it is in "at-onement," as I am calling it, in being at one, that is, with others and with myself, that I found my moment of peace, of timelessness, that I discovered for myself the intersection of time and eternity. In passing over to the people from the hammocks I was entering into a sharing of life, and so it is no wonder that I found at-onement. In passing over to the people from the cabins, on the other hand, I was entering into a loneliness, a feeling of separation. Still, it was *saudade*, a longing based on human ties. So there too I found at-onement. When I came back to myself, however, I was reentering my own loneliness, my own feeling of separation, and that was a longing based on a lack of human ties, it seemed to me as I contrasted my background with that of the others, the indefinite longing of an individual who is thrown back upon himself and who lives in the solitude of his own heart.

I found at-onement there too, nevertheless, coming back to myself instead of being thrown back upon myself, and now I can see how eternity passes through time in the heart's longing as well as in the actual sharing of life, and in the indefinite longing that arises in the solitude of the heart as well as in the longing that arises from actual human ties. Eternity is connected with the person who lives the life just as time is connected with the life that the person lives. Eternity appears when person merges with person, whether I merge with another or with myself. It is the missing dimension of depth, of timelessness that gives depth to time, in a "flatland,"[4] as in Edwin Abbott's story, where persons are like circles who cannot see inside each other. It appears when we do become able to see inside, when instead of simply meeting we pass over and come back, like circles turning on their axes and becoming spheres.

If the human essence comes to light in at-onement, in our oneness with one another and with ourselves, it is connected with the depth of timelessness in time. It is our kinship with the Eternal, our capacity for a relationship with God. When I pass over to people who share life with one another like those from the hammocks, I find the human essence in my oneness with them and their oneness with one another, and when I come back to myself, I find it in my own oneness with myself. When I pass over to people who long for their oneness like those from the cabins, I find it in their longing just as I find it, when I come back to myself, in my own longing. I can see in the oneness how the human essence is to be found in relationship with others and with oneself, not just with others in "the ensemble of the social relations"[5] as Marx saw it or in man and woman together as Freud saw it but with oneself as well as with others. I can see in the longing, moreover, that the human essence is in the very capacity for relationship, but it is eclipsed when there is no actual relatedness. If time is onward flow and eternity is timeless depth, this infinite capacity of ours is the sea, this inexhaustible capacity of mind and heart.

God then is not this sea itself but is light pervading this infinite sea, light illumining the mind and kindling the heart. "God has no essence,"[6] I concluded, no limiting essence, I meant, thinking of the human essence in the individual, in man and woman together, in "the ensemble of the social relations," for God is present not only where the human essence is present but also throughout the universe. God's "essence," if we speak of it, as in creeds saying God has "one essence,"[7] is something that appears in a oneness with all beings. There is no being in all the universe, that is, to which

God is alien, and the human essence opens out upon infinity, is permeable by the light that God is. God clashes with the unrelatedness, though, even of one human being with another. It is there in unrelatedness, in separation, that I find the true "heart of darkness."[8]

At the Church of the Poor Devil, at the end of our riverboat voyage up the Amazon, I thought I might be encountering some kind of "heart of darkness" as in Conrad's story of a riverboat voyage up the Congo. I thought at first the little chapel might have something to do with devil-worship, and later when I returned for the festival and learned of its connection with African religion I had a similar feeling. As it turned out, though, I discovered there something rather like light shining in the darkness, like the candles people lit and placed before the chapel at night. I found there the religion of the poor, the religion of the people in the huts along the river and of the people from the hammocks on the riverboat. I found not only their sharing of life, as I had on the riverboat, but also their heart's desire, the deep longing that is imaged in the burning candles and in the very structure of the chapel itself. When I tried to pass over, to enter into the religion of the poor, as I had into their sharing of life, I became aware of my own starting point, as I had of the solitude and the longing of my own heart. I became aware of personal religion.

I realized I was passing over from the desire in my own heart to that in the heart of the poor. As I went from story to story about the Church of the Poor Devil, from that of its being built by a poor workingman, the first story I came upon, to that of its being the fulfillment of a *promessa* to Santo Antonio, the story that proved to be true, I found myself meditating on heart's desire and human needs. There is a connection, I can see, of human needs with time and of heart's desire with eternity: human needs have to do with the persons and the situations belonging to a life, entering the life and passing from the life, and heart's desire has to do with the relatedness a person has to the things of life, merging with the persons and with self in the situations of life. To follow my heart's desire is to walk through life upright, like the vertical dimension passing through the horizontal, instead of being dragged through by my needs.

To pass over to the heart's desire of the poor, however, is to go over to "the sigh of the oppressed creature," as Marx describes religion, "the heart of a heartless world, and the soul of soulless conditions."[9] The interior of the Church of the Poor Devil is an image of that heart and that soul, a still and empty place, a zero point where the vertical dimension of eternity intersects the horizontal dimension of time, a void of the imagination where grace can come in like light flowing down into the dark. The inner space of the chapel, to be sure, is filled by imagination with saints, as I found, corresponding to African gods and goddesses, but there is a way leading from the many to the one, from the many human needs to the one heart's desire. It is in making that passage from the many to the one that I come to the sigh, the heart and the soul of the poor. I go from the complexity of human needs to the simplicity of heart's desire in the poor as in myself. What I find at the intersection point of time and eternity is how human needs are pervaded by heart's desire, how the sigh of the poor is also my sigh, how the heart and soul of the poor is also my heart and soul.

If I set aside the judgment Marx passes on the religion of the poor, that it is "the opium of the people," and let myself be led by the heart's desire, I find I have joined the poor on their journey in time. To follow their sigh, their heart and their soul, is to walk upright through time rather than be dragged as an oppressed creature through a heartless world by soulless conditions of life. The vertical dimension transforms the horizontal as it passes through, takes away the oppressiveness, the heartlessness, the soullessness of the "flatland." If I follow the sigh, the heart and the soul of the poor, I follow my own deepest longing. "God is the heart's desire,"[10] I concluded, not the longing itself but what we are longing for, and to follow the heart's desire is to be led by God on our journey in time. God leads by heart and mind, and to follow God's lead is to take the way, insight by insight, of the kindling of heart and the illumining of mind.

Is there really a way of heart's desire, a way of freeing the oppressed, of giving heart to the world, of endowing the conditions of life with soul? At the festival I seemed to see an answer to the prayer, "Show us the way!" I seemed to see the way shown in image as we walked in procession from the Church of the Poor Devil into the night with our lighted candles. The light of our candles suggested the light shining in the darkness, the light kindling hearts and illumining minds. Our sharing the light, lighting each other's candles and relighting them when they blew out in the wind, suggested the giving and receiving of insight. Our faces illumined by the light of our candles as we walked and sang, our seeing all faces other than our own, suggested our knowing one another in the light of mind and heart and our knowing ourselves in being known by one another. Our coming in the end into the large and lighted space of the Church of Santa Rita, and the hymn we sang there of "eternal vision" (*eternal visão*), suggested the goal and the continuity of the way and the goal, that an eternal knowing and being known is the goal and each insight along the way, each kindling of heart and illumining of mind, is a taste of that eternity.

A way of heart and mind, of kindling and illumining, can be a way of freeing the oppressed, if oppression itself is essentially a matter of knowing and not knowing, of being known and not being known. I think here of Hegel on the masters and the slaves,[11] seeing the masters as those who are recognized but do not recognize and the slaves as those who recognize but are not recognized in their selfhood. Mastery and slavery are abolished, according to this, only in the mutuality of knowing and being known. They remain there, the archetypes of a world in continual conflict, through change after change in society, as long as the basic human relations of knowing and being known are left unchanged. It is only on a way like that imaged on the night of our festival, it seems, a way of giving and receiving light, of coming to know and be known, that "the invisible man"[12] ever becomes visible, that the face of a person who lives in shadows ever becomes illumined.

It is knowing and being known in the heart's longing that gives heart to a heartless world, I want to say, and it is knowing and being known in the conditions of life, if they are not separated from the heart's longing, that gives soul to soulless conditions. I think of the woman of the *favela* telling of the conditions of her life and of her heart's longing in her diary. Her starting point is the *favela*, "the garbage dump"[13] as she calls it, and her goal is escape from the *favela*, "the brick house" that is her dream, and her way goes from the one to the other. Actually following the way, though, changes her perception both of the starting point and of the goal, and she ends by embracing poverty as a way, the very way of Christ. So it is the conditions of life that determine our starting point and the heart's longing that determines our goal, but they do so ever more truly as they become ever more luminous in knowing and being known. As we walk the way, step by step, we come to the wisdom that arises, insight by insight, out of suffering, out of the clash between the heart's longing and the actual conditions of life, out of truthfulness to heart's desire and to human misery.

"Eternal vision" itself is a wisdom that comes from suffering, it seems, a knowing and being known that arises out of living an entire life. As we live we come, if we are willing, to know and be known, like the woman of the *favela*, in our naked humanity. I think of Rouault setting images of suffering humanity side by side with images of the suffering Christ. "The way is that of knowing and being known in our naked humanity,"[14] I concluded, a way not simply of suffering, I meant, but of passing over to others in their suffering, a way of acting upon insight into suffering. As we walk upright through time, eternity is revealed in time—that is the knowing and being known. As we go from the complexity of meeting our needs to the simplicity of following our heart's desire, we are stripped to our bare humanity, and we are revealed to one another and to ourselves, and God and our capacity for God is revealed.

What I am coming to here, I can see as I stand back and reflect, is not simply a vision of human misery, where heart's desire is taken to be an illusion, where suffering calls forth only a system of meeting human needs. Nor is it simply a vision of heart's desire, where misery is taken to be something ephemeral, where wisdom is thought to consist in being able to say, even in the direst need, "I lack nothing." Rather it is a vision of the human road, of the path in time that opens up before us when we acknowledge the truth both of human misery and of heart's desire. Human misery is connected with time, I can see, and heart's desire with eternity. To dismiss heart's desire as an illusion is to say time alone is real; to dismiss human misery as something ephemeral is to say eternity alone is real. To acknowledge the truth of both is to see the intersection of time and eternity in the moment. It is there at the point where the vertical dimension meets the horizontal that I can see the human road opening up before us. The human road is the path of eternity in time, of the vertical dimension passing through the horizontal, of the human being walking upright.

Ahead of us the human road disappears from view, something that is surprising when we think of human misery as our starting point and heart's desire as our goal, for it would seem possible simply to draw a line from where we are to where we are going and call that our path. It is not surprising, though, when we think of human misery in terms of time as a horizontal and heart's desire in terms of eternity as a vertical dimension, for then we stand in this moment where human misery already meets heart's desire but we do not yet stand in that moment ahead. Here and now, the moment where we are, is the starting point when we think of it simply as a point in time, a point where human misery is not yet alleviated. It foreshadows the goal, though, when we think of it as a point of intersection with eternity, a point where heart's desire is already present. Ahead of us, where the road disappears from view, beyond our "already" and "not yet," is the point of no return.

There is no return, I mean, as in passing over to others and returning again to oneself. Whenever I start from my own starting point, the longing that arises in the solitude of my own heart, and pass over into a sharing of life or into a longing that arises out of human ties, I always return again to the solitude of my own heart. When I start from our common starting point, on the other hand, the misery of the human condition, and seek to go from there to our common goal, the fulfillment of our heart's desire, I am seeking to find a point of no return, a point where we can rest in heartsease without coming back again to human misery. There is a correspondence between that point and my own starting point, between the fulfillment of our heart's desire and the longing of my own heart. That appears even more clearly when I see how my own longing, and the longing that arises out of human ties, and the sigh, the heart and the soul of the poor are all forms of "the love that moves the sun and the other stars,"[15] the love that pervades the universe. The vertical dimension of eternity, I can see, pervades the horizontal dimension of time at all points, and every point in time is able to be the happy ending of time.

All we know of the happy ending, nevertheless, is what we learn in a moment of vision, as when I saw the richness of life on the riverboat or the stillness and emptiness inside the chapel of the Poor Devil or the light shining in the darkness on the night of the festival. "Only God," I concluded, "can see the human road through to the end."[16] For we always come back to ourselves again from moments of vision. I always come back to myself. I must or I will suffer the interior catastrophe that occurs when one passes over and does not come back, the loss of personal existence, the loss of the standpoint of personal religion, the loss of one's way on the personal journey in life. Only death, it seems, can be the point where there is no more coming back, where vision does not pass, and that may be because death is the final coming to oneself. Anyway, coming back to myself can be a moment of vision too, when I find my own eyes and heart.

Is it really possible, I ask when I find my own eyes and heart, to see what others see, by passing over, and even to see what God sees, by coming back, to see at least that God sees the human road through to the end? ("Who made the eyes but I?" Love asks in George Herbert's poem.)[17] Is it really possible, that is, to share in the knowledge and love of others, and even in that of God? Here I come upon Plato's alternatives: No sharing of one in another? Or that of all in all? Or that of some in some?[18]

"No sharing of one in another"—that is how things look when I stand off myself from participation in humanity, when I have differentiated myself from my lot in life but have found no way of being heart and soul with the persons and in the situations of my life. It is then that the course of human events appears to be devoid of God, of eternity, of any love "with all your heart, and with all your soul, and with all your might."[19] There is instead the inhumanity of one human being to another. Human events are devoid, I would have said without reflecting, of God's love for us, of God's intervention to prevent evil among us, but in reality they are devoid, I see as I reflect on it, of our love of God, of our being heart and soul in our lives with one another, devoid actually of my love of God, for it is I who stand aloof at this point, who have not made the lover's choice to live with all my heart and soul, to participate fully in humanity. What holds me back, I see as I reflect further, what makes me incapable of love, is my unwillingness to undergo pain, to be heart and soul with persons and in situations to my loss.

"All in all"—that is how things look when I do make the lover's choice to love with all my heart, and with all my soul, and with all my might, all time in eternity and all eternity in time. God is at work in the course of human events through the mind and heart of our knowing and loving, it appears to me now, and yet we are able to live and love with all our heart, and with all our soul, and with all our might only in relation to God. I add "mind" as the command is phrased in the Gospels, to love "with all your heart, and with all your soul, and with all your mind, and with all your strength,"[20] so as to join the knowing and the loving. "All in all" so understood, I believe, is God's will according to "Faith in God" (*Fé em Deus*), the words I saw over the door of a hut on the Amazon. When the will of God is being "done on earth as it is in heaven," there is an "all in all." Not everything that happens in human affairs, though, is in accord with the will of God. Instead of "all in all" there is "some in some."

"Some in some," therefore—that is how things look when I see the inhumanity of one human being to another, when I see how God's will is not always done, how "God is vulnerable,"[21] how God suffers in those who are suffering and is in conflict with those who are doing injustice. Now I come from the vision of loving with all my mind and with all my heart to that of knowing with God's mind and loving with God's heart. "God is there in all we know and love," I concluded, "but in the knowing and the loving."[22] When I am heart and soul, mind and strength in loving God, I am sharing in humanity, finding human wholeness in relation to God. When I am seeing human suffering and feeling the inhumanity of one human being to another, on the other hand, I am sharing in divinity, seeing with God's eyes and feeling with God's heart. I can see in the image of the suffering Christ how sharing in humanity, entering heart and soul into human existence, leads to sharing in divinity, to becoming vulnerable with God's own vulnerability to human injustice and human suffering. I can see what it means if God says of the Church of the Poor Devil, as he says of the Temple, "my eyes and my heart will be there for all time."[23] I realize at last how daring it is to ask for God's eyes and heart.

I see a happy ending, nevertheless, when I see with those eyes and that heart; I see a divine comedy like Dante's where everything converges like a white rose upon its center. At first I was seeing all human beings in a great circle, each of us located at some point on the circle by the conditions of our life, with heart's desire at the center, the goal of our journey, and radial paths coming from every point on the circle to the center, the converging way of heart's desire. Then later I was seeing Christ at the center and seeing our way leading us, by radial paths of personal destiny, from where we are to where Christ is. Now I am seeing where we are as where eternity is passing through our time, as we walk upright, moving toward the center where Christ is, as we follow Christ in time. We are like Peter in *Quo Vadis*,[24] meeting Christ on our own road, walking toward the ending of our hope and of our fear.

I have been talking of the Church of the Poor Devil as an image of religion of the poor. I have been speaking in a parable. Now I want to interpret my parable and say, *Christianity is the true religion of the poor.* It is the sigh that expresses the true longing of the oppressed creature, I mean, the heart that can change a heartless world, the soul that can free us from soulless conditions. It does not change the things of life; it changes our relationship to the things; and so it changes our relationship with one another. It can change even "the ensemble of the social relations."

Where then is the human essence? It is in "the ensemble of the social relations," I found, as among the people on the riverboat; it is in man and woman together like Antonio and Cordolina; it is in the individual like me passing over to all of them and coming back again to myself. Where is the heart's desire? It is in turning on the axis of our own human existence, I found, while orbiting around the sun of divine existence, as in the promise that built the Church of the Poor Devil. Which is the human way? It is not simply the way of suffering, I found; it is the way of wisdom that comes from suffering "by the awful grace of God,"[25] like the light illumining our way on the night of the festival; it is the way of following that wisdom, like us following our light to the place where we sang of "eternal vision." Who can see the way? Not I nor those to whom I passed over, I concluded, but only God, if seeing the way means seeing it through to the end. What then of God? Where is God in all the suffering endured by the poor and the hungry and the sorrowful and the outcast? God is there in the suffering and the longing, I concluded, but God's presence is felt in the illumining and the kindling, in the knowing and the loving.

There is a kinship among all these questions I have been asking, I can see, where the human essence is, where the heart's desire is, where the human way is going, where the road disappears from view, where God is, and now where time intersects with eternity. There is one answer to all of them. "We all have within us a center of stillness surrounded by silence,"[26] Hammarskjold says, introducing the Meditation Room at the United Nations. I can say the same, speaking of the Church of the Poor Devil. There is a center of stillness there, and there is a center of stillness within us. Passing over to the religion of the poor means going over to the center of stillness that is imaged there. Coming back to personal religion means coming back to the center of stillness that is within us. Passing over and coming back is the way, not force or inertia; the center of stillness is the goal, reached and yet to be reached. Eternity walks upright through time.

NOTES

Notes to the Preface

1. Karl Marx, *Critique of Hegel's Philosophy of Right*, ed. Joseph O'Malley (Cambridge: Cambridge University Press, 1970), p. 131.
2. Plato, *Timaeus* 37d (my translation).
3. Cf. his works cited in chapter 2, note 51.

Notes to Chapter One

1. Here is my log of our voyage. Our riverboat was the Lobo d'Almada, actually a "twin-screw motorship" with accommodations for 398 passengers, according to *Lloyd's Register of Shipping 1978–79* (London, Lloyd's, 1978), vol. 2, p. 129. Our voyage began at Belém on Wednesday, July 26, 1978, at 10:00 A.M. We came to Almeirim at 5:15 P.M. on Thursday, to Monte Alegre at 7:45 A.M., and to Santarem at 2:35 P.M. (time moved back an hour) on Friday, to Obidos at 3:00 A.M. and to Parintins at 1:30 P.M. on Saturday. We arrived at Manaus on Sunday, July 30, at 5:00 P.M.
2. Karl Marx, *Theses on Feuerbach*, Thesis 6 in Karl Marx and Friedrich Engels, *Basic Writings on Politics and Philosophy*, ed. Lewis S. Feuer (Garden City, N.Y.: Doubleday, 1959), p. 244.
3. Marx, *Theses*, Thesis 3.
4. Dag Hammarskjold, *Markings*, trans. Leif Sjoberg and W. H. Auden (New York: Knopf, 1964), p. 157.
5. Joseph Conrad, *Heart of Darkness* (New York: Penguin, 1978), p. 39.
6. Alexis de Tocqueville, *Democracy in America*, trans. Henry Reeve, revised by Francis Bowen, ed. Phillips Bradley (New York: Vintage, 1959), vol. 2, p. 106.
7. John Donne, Meditation 17 from "Devotions upon Emergent Occasions" in *Complete Poetry and Selected Prose*, ed. John Hayward (New York: Random House, 1929), p. 538.
8. Theodor Haecker, *Journal in the Night*, trans. Alexander Dru (London:

Harvill Press, 1949), p. 38.

9. Robert Louis Stevenson, "An Apology for Idlers" in *The Works of Robert Louis Stevenson*, Vailima edition, vol. 2 (New York: Scribners, 1922), p. 94.

10. Marx, *Theses*, Thesis 6.

11. Genesis 1:27. Here and throughout, unless otherwise indicated, I use the Revised Standard Version (Old Testament 1952 and New Testament 1972).

12. Herbert Read, *The Green Child* (London: Eyre and Spottiswoode, 1947), pp. 149f.

13. Apparently the story refers to the four caravels led by Vincente Yáñez Pinzón, who discovered the mouth of the Amazon in 1500 and was so impressed by the wide expanse of fresh water at the mouth that he named the river Santa Maria de la Mar Dulce.

14. Conrad, p. 89.

15. Ibid., p. 94 ("You will be lost . . . ") and p. 100 ("The horror . . . ").

16. Ibid., p. 101.

17. Ibid., p. 87 ("the image of its own tenebrous and passionate soul"), p. 102 ("a soul as translucently pure as a cliff of crystal"), and pp. 95f. ("But his soul was mad. . . . I saw the inconceivable mystery of a soul that knew no restraint, no faith, and no fear, yet struggling blindly with itself").

18. Cf. Sebastian Brant, *The Ship of Fools* (*Das Narrenschiff*, 1497) trans. Edwin H. Zeydel (New York: Dover, 1944). Cf. also Katherine Anne Porter's *Ship of Fools* (Boston: Little, Brown & Co., 1962), p. vii.

19. Hammarskjold, *Markings*, p. 87.

20. Conrad, p. 31.

21. Deuteronomy 6:5. Cf. also Matthew 22:37, Mark 12:30, and Luke 10:27.

22. Dante, *Paradiso*, 31: 91–93. Here and throughout I am using and translating from the edition by Paget Toynbee, *Le opere di Dante Alighieri* (Oxford: Oxford University Press, 1924). Cf. my discussion of this passage in *The Reasons of the Heart* (New York: Macmillan, 1978), pp. 111ff.

23. Cf. my discussion of loneliness becoming a longing for communion with God in *The Reasons of the Heart*, pp. 3ff.

24. J.R.R. Tolkien, *The Lord of the Rings*, one-volume edition (London: George Allen & Unwin, 1969), p. 103.

25. W. B. Yeats, *A Vision* (New York: Collier, 1966), p. 136.

26. Yeats says of Shelley, "He lacked the Vision of Evil, could not conceive of the world as a continual conflict," ibid., p. 144.

27. Ibid., pp. 136f. Cf. also ibid., p. 285 ("the inadequacy of man's fate to

man" and "man's inadequacy to his fate").

28. Cf. note 8.
29. James Joyce's *Finnegans Wake* (New York; Viking, 1959) ends with the words "A way a lone a last a loved a long the" and it begins with the word "riverrun." The book makes a complete circle, that is, and tries to do what Alcmaeon says men cannot do, "join the beginning to the end."
30. Katherine Anne Porter, *Ship of Fools*, p. vii.
31. William Vaughn Moody, "The Death of Eve" in *The Poems and Plays of William Vaughn Moody* (Boston and New York: Houghton Mifflin, 1912), vol. 1, p. 445.
32. Plato, *Republic* 6, 509b in *The Dialogues of Plato* trans. Benjamin Jowett (New York: Random House, 1937), vol. 1, p. 770. When Socrates uttered this statement, "Glaucon said, with a ludicrous earnestness: 'By the light of heaven, how amazing!' "
33. Cf. Aquinas, *De Ente et Essentia* ed. C. Boyer (Rome: Gregoriana, 1946), p. 43 ("Deus non habet quidditatem vel essentiam"). (Aquinas is quoting Avicenna here, *Metaphysica*, 8, ch. 4, "Primus igitur non habet quidditatem," ibid., note 89). Aquinas was willing to say "God has no essence," meaning God's essence is none other than God's existence. I am saying it in what I think is an equivalent way, meaning God is not confined to our relationship with God.
34. Dante, *Paradiso*, 33, 145 (the last line of *The Divine Comedy*).
35. Moody, "The Death of Eve," p. 436.
36. Alcmaeon, Fragment 2, trans. Kathleen Freeman in *Ancilla to the Pre-Socratic Philosophers* (Cambridge, Mass.: Harvard University Press, 1957), p. 40.

Notes to Chapter Two

1. Cf. John Brooks, ed., *The South American Handbook* (Bath, England: Trade & Travel Publications, 1977), p. 277. The present *zeladora* (woman caretaker) of the chapel also mentioned this story to me and said the workingman's name was Francisco.
2. Vera Kelsey, *Brazil in Capitals* (New York and London: Harper, 1942), p. 159.
3. Bertita Harding, *Southern Empire* (New York: Coward-McCann, 1948), p. 142.
4. Gastão de Bettencourt in João de Barros, José Osório de Oliveira, Gastão de Bettencourt, *Brasil* (Lisbon: Edicões Europa, 1938), p. 348.
5. I am going here on a copy of the deed that Geraldo Pinheiro photocopied

for me and a transcript of a tape-recorded conversation between Geraldo Pinheiro and an old black woman named Mundica Charuto who actually knew Cordolina (here is where I learned that Cordolina used to call herself "the Poor Devil") and my conversations with Geraldo Pinheiro, with his brother Padre Raimundo Nonato Pinheiro (he told me of a sign Antonio had at his place showing a grotesque figure and reading *Ao Pobre Diabo* and how people used to ask Antonio "Are you the devil?" and Antonio would answer "No, I am the Poor Devil"—cf. also his article in the Manaus newspaper *A Noticia* for January 22, 1978), and with Mario Ypiranga Monteiro (he also spoke of the sign at Antonio's place but added that Cordolina afterward had a sign at her place reading *A Pobre Diaba*—cf. his article on Pobre Diabo in his "Roteiro Historico de Manaus" in the Manaus newspaper *A Critica* for September 14, 1969).

6. Karl Marx, *Critique of Hegel's Philosophy of Right*, ed. Joseph O'Malley (Cambridge: Cambridge University Press, 1970), p. 131.

7. Le Corbusier [Edouard Jeanneret-Gris], *Towards a New Architecture*, trans. Frederick Etchells (New York: Payson & Clarke, 1927), p. 153, repeated on p. 203.

8. Ibid., p. 72.

9. Sigmund Freud, *The Future of an Illusion*, trans. W.D. Robson-Scott (New York: Doubleday, 1964).

10. Marx, *Critique*, p. 131.

11. Soren Kierkegaard, *Concluding Unscientific Postscript*, trans. David Swenson and Walter Lowrie (Princeton: Princeton University Press, 1941), p. 527.

12. A tape-recorded conversation in 1969 between Geraldo Pinheiro and an old black woman named Mundica Charuto who lived in the neighborhood of the Church of the Poor Devil and knew Cordolina.

13. There is a song in Afro-Brazilian dialect:

Santatonho catungado	Santo Antonio the matchmaker
Ere mora na aruana. . .	He lives in heaven. . .
Ai! Ere mora na aruana	Ah! He lives in heaven
E vem casa fia de ubana. . . .	And he comes to marry daughters of the earth. . . .

It is quoted by Gastão de Bettencourt, *Os Três Santos de Junho no Folclore Brasílico* (Rio de Janeiro: AGIR, 1947), p. 71.

14. W. B. Yeats, *A Vision* (New York: Collier, 1966), pp. 140f.

15. Soren Kierkegaard, *Purity of Heart Is to Will One Thing*, trans. Douglas V. Steere (New York: Harper & Row, 1965).

16. Le Corbusier [Edouard Jeanneret-Gris], *The Chapel at Ronchamp* (New

York: Frederick A. Praeger, 1957), p. 88.

17. Bernard Pomerance, *The Elephant Man* (New York: Grove, 1979), p. 38.

18. Cf. Abraham Maslow's "hierarchy of needs": physiological needs, safety, love and belonging, esteem, and self-actualization, described in his book *Motivation and Personality* (New York: Harper, 1954), pp. 80ff.

19. Theodore Roethke, "The Right Thing" in *The Far Field* (Garden City, N.Y.: Doubleday, 1964), p. 94.

20. Marx, *Critique*, p. 132.

21. Alexis de Tocqueville, *Democracy in America*, trans. Henry Reeve, revised by Francis Bowen, ed. Phillips Bradley (New York: Vintage, 1959), vol. 2, p. 106.

22. Yeats, *A Vision*, pp. 140f.

23. Le Corbusier, *The Chapel at Ronchamp*, p. 129.

24. Cf. Karl Jaspers, *Philosophy*, trans. E.B. Ashton, vol. 2 (Chicago and London: University of Chicago Press, 1970), p. 178. Cf. my discussion of these situations in *The Reasons of the Heart* (New York: Macmillan, 1978), pp. 21ff.

25. Albert Camus, *The Myth of Sisyphus*, trans. Justin O'Brien (New York: Vintage, 1955), p. 91.

26. Marx, *Critique*, p. 131.

27. John Keats, letter to George and Georgina Keats, Sunday, 14 February to Monday, 3 May, 1819, in *The Letters of John Keats*, ed. Maurice Buxton Forman (London: Oxford University Press, 1948), pp. 336f.

28. Le Corbusier, *The Chapel at Ronchamp*, p. 25.

29. Descartes, *Discourse on Method*, trans. John Veitch in *The Rationalists* (Garden City, N.Y.: Doubleday, 1961), p. 57. Cf. my discussion of this maxim in *The Way of All the Earth* (New York: Macmillan, 1972), p. 162.

30. W.B. Yeats, *Collected Poems* (New York: Macmillan, 1956), p. 197.

31. I realize this is not the usual conception of magic and science and religion. Cf. my earlier discussion in *The City of the Gods* (New York: Macmillan, 1965), pp. 119ff. On the *anima hominis* and the *anima mundi* cf. W.B. Yeats, *Per Amica Silentia Lunae* (New York: Macmillan, 1918) where these terms are the titles of the two parts of the book (pp. 17 and 51).

32. Le Corbusier, *The Chapel at Ronchamp*, p. 27. Cf. also ibid., p. 95 ("Light flows down").

33. Dag Hammarskjold, "A Room of Quiet: The United Nations Meditation Room," reprinted in Dag Hammarskjold, *Servant of Peace*, ed. Wilder Foote (London: The Bodley Head, 1962), p. 161.

34. Robert Browning, *Poetical Works 1833–64*, ed. Ian Jack (London: Oxford University Press, 1970), p. 614.

35. On Yeats rebuilding Thoor Ballylee see T. R. Henn, *The Lonely Tower*

(London: Methuen, 1965). On Carl Gustav Jung building Bollingen see his autobiography, *Memories, Dreams, Reflections*, ed. Aniela Jaffe and trans. Richard and Clara Winston (New York: Vintage, 1963), pp. 223ff.

36. When I visited Zulmira with Geraldo Pinheiro, I learned there were three kinds of Afro-Brazilian rites practiced in her place: *candomblé*, *umbanda*, and *macumba*, but Zulmira spoke particularly of *umbanda*. The best authority on these rites is Roger Bastide, *The African Religions of Brazil*, trans. Helen Sebba (Baltimore and London: Johns Hopkins University Press, 1978). Cf. also his table of saints and gods in *African Civilizations in the New World*, trans. Peter Green (New York: Harper & Row, 1971), pp. 157f. Zulmira told me the chief celebrations in her place were those of Santa Barbara, São Benedito (depicted as black), and São Sebastião. I asked her particularly about the goddess Jemanja (Yemanja) whose picture was on the wall across from the replica of the chapel and who had a whole room devoted to her worship in the *barracão*. Zulmira told me that Jemanja corresponded to Nossa Senhora da Conceição and was goddess of the waters.

37. Le Corbusier, *The Chapel at Ronchamp*, p. 27 ("the play of proportions. . . ") and p. 47 ("Observe the play. . . ").

38. Le Corbusier, *Towards a New Architecture*, p. 5.

39. Simone Weil, *Gravity and Grace*, trans. Arthur Wills (New York: Putnam, 1952), p. 62.

40. Plato, *Timaeus*, 37d (my translation).

41. G.W.F. Hegel, *Phenomenology of Mind*, trans. James Baillie (New York: Macmillan, 1961), p. 237.

42. Cf. my discussion of Hegel's idea of self-realization through work in *The Reasons of the Heart*, p. 126.

43. Elie Wiesel, *Night*, trans. Stella Rodway (New York: Avon, 1969), p. 51.

44. I John 4:18.

45. John 9:4 (King James Version).

46. Dag Hammarskjold, *Markings*, trans. Leif Sjoberg and W.H. Auden (New York: Knopf, 1964), p. 159 (cf. p. 37 for the first quotation of "Night is drawing nigh" and W.H. Auden's note on the Swedish hymn from which it is taken).

47. Genesis 1:2.

48. Soren Kierkegaard, *The Concept of Dread*, trans. by Walter Lowrie (Princeton: Princeton University Press, 1957), p. 139 ("a saving experience. . . ") and p. 142 ("lighter now. . . ").

49. From the poem "The Phases of the Moon" in Yeats, *A Vision*, p. 60.

50. Simone Weil, *Waiting for God*, trans. Emma Craufurd (New York: Putnam, 1951), p. 67.

51. Diego Irarrazaval, "Cristo Morado: Señor de los maltratados," *Paginas* (Lima, Peru), vol. 3, no. 13 (December 1977), p. 31. Cf. also his book, *Religion del Pobre y Liberacion* (Lima, Peru: Centro de Estudios y Publicaciones, 1978) and in collaboration with Maximiliano Salinas, *Hacia una Teologia de los Pobres* (Lima, Peru: Centro de Estudios y Publicaciones, 1980).

52. Le Corbusier, *The Chapel at Ronchamp*, p. 103.

53. From the *Ave Maria*. We said it over and over again, as we recited the rosary, each night in the Church of the Poor Devil during the novena in preparation for the festival of Santo Antonio.

54. Weil, *Waiting for God*, p. 67.

55. Cf. Franz Cumont, *Lux Perpetua* (Paris: Libraire Orientaliste Paul Geuthner, 1949).

56. Bettencourt, p. 348.

57. Soren Kierkegaard, *The Sickness unto Death*, trans. Walter Lowrie (London: Oxford University Press, 1941), p. 23.

58. Cf. chapter 1, section 2.

59. Weil, *Waiting on God*, p. 66.

60. Yeats, *A Vision*, pp. 136f. ("forerunner" and "successor") and p. 285 ("inadequacy" and "fate"). The terminology here corresponds to that quoted above in chapter 1, note 27, "man's inadequacy to his fate" to "the unworthiness of man to his lot," and "the inadequacy of man's fate to man" to "the unworthiness of man's lot to man."

61. Ibid., p. 285.

62. Cf. Camus, *The Myth of Sisyphus*, p. 90.

63. F. W. Nietzsche, *Thus Spake Zarathustra*, trans. Walter Kaufmann in *The Portable Nietzsche* (New York: Viking, 1954), p. 340.

64. Juliana of Norwich, *Showings*, trans. Edmund Colledge and James Walsh (New York: Paulist Press, 1978), p. 225.

65. Le Corbusier, *The Chapel at Ronchamp*, p. 24.

66. John 1:5.

67. Juliana of Norwich, p. 225.

68. Jung, *Memories, Dreams, Reflections*, p. 280.

69. This is the chorus of a hymn to Santo Antonio with ten stanzas, "Exulta berço glorioso."

70. John Henry Newman, "Lead Kindly Light" in *A Newman Reader*, ed. Francis X. Connelly (Garden City, N.Y.: Image, 1964), pp. 74f.

71. Yeats, *A Vision*, pp. 284f.

72. Vittorio Lanternari, *The Religions of the Oppressed*, trans. Lisa Sergio (New York: Knopf, 1963).

73. On this idea of "the things of life" and "the relation to the things" see my book *Time and Myth* (Garden City, N.Y.: Doubleday, 1973), pp. 12ff.

74. Rainer Maria Rilke, *Stories of God*, trans. M. D. Herter Norton (New York: Norton, 1963), pp. 33ff.
75. Rainer Maria Rilke, *Letters to a Young Poet*, trans. M. D. Herter Norton (New York: Norton, 1962), p. 49.

Notes to Chapter Three

1. The song cited above in chapter 2, note 69.
2. Martin Buber, *The Way of Man* (Chicago: Cloister Press, 1951), pp. 15ff.
3. J.R.R. Tolkien, *The Lord of the Rings*, one-volume edition (London: George Allen & Unwin, 1969), p. 87.
4. John 1:4.
5. Karl Marx, *Critique of the Gotha Programme* ed. C. P. Dutt (New York: International Publishers, 1938), p. 10.
6. Gastão de Bettencourt in João de Barros, José Osório de Oliveira, Gastão de Bettencourt, *Brasil* (Lisbon: Edicoes Europe, 1938), p. 348.
7. Carolina Maria de Jesus, *Child of the Dark* trans. David St. Clair (New York: New American Library, 1963), p. 148 (cf. also p. 67). The saints of June are Santo Antonio (June 13), São João (June 24), and São Pedro (June 29). Cf. Bettencourt, *Os Três Santos de Junho* cited in chapter 2, note 13.
8. Luke 6:20–22.
9. Aeschylus, *Agamemnon*, trans. Edith Hamilton, *Three Greek Plays* (New York: Norton, 1937), p. 170.
10. Georges Rouault, *Miserere* (Boston: Boston Book & Art Shop with the Trianon Press, 1963), Plates 3 (Christ "forever scourged") and 18 ("The condemned is led away"). I am retranslating the French titles.
11. Max Frisch, *I'm Not Stiller* trans. Michael Bullock (London and New York: Abelard-Schuman, 1958), p. 335.
12. Rouault, *Miserere*, Plate 55.
13. Carolina Maria de Jesus, *Child of the Dark*, p. 156.
14. Dag Hammarskjold, *Markings*, trans. Leif Sjoberg and W. H. Auden (New York: Knopf, 1964), p. 89.
15. Carolina Maria de Jesus, *Child of the Dark*, p. 29 ("I am very happy. . . ."), p. 40 ("How horrible it is. . . ."), p. 47 ("She looked at the *favela*. . . .").
16. John 1:5
17. Romans 4:18 ("In hope he believed against hope").
18. John 9:3.
19. Hammarskjold, *Markings*, p. 166.

20. "Vive-se melhor sendo pobre do que sendo rico. Talvez seja por isso que Jesus Cristo perferiu ser pobre" quoted in *Ebony*, vol. 22 (December 1966), p. 104.

21. 1 Kings 3:9.

22. Ezechiel 24:16.

23. Fyodor Dostoevsky, *Crime and Punishment* trans. Constance Garnett (New York: Random House, 1944), p. 319.

24. Cf. Paulo Freire, *The Pedagogy of the Oppressed* trans. Myra Bergman Ramos (New York: Seabury, 1970), pp. 19ff.

25. Cf. G.W.F. Hegel, *Phenomenology of Mind*, trans. James Baillie (New York: Macmillan, 1961), p. 237.

26. Frisch, p. 335.

27. Jeremiah 10:23.

28. Michael Polanyi, *Personal Knowledge* (New York: Harper Torchbooks, 1964), p. x.

29. Augustine, *Soliloquies*, Book 2, ch. 1, ed. Thomas F. Gilligan (New York: Cosmopolitan Science & Art Service Co., 1943), p. 70 ("noverim me, noverim te") (my translation).

30. Loren Eiseley, *The Night Country* (New York: Scribner's, 1971), p. 159.

31. W.B. Yeats, *A Vision* (New York: Collier, 1966), p. 111.

32. Carolina Maria de Jesus, *Child of the Dark*, p. 128.

33. Rouault, *Miserere*, Plate 13.

34. Psalm 34:8.

35. Carolina Maria de Jesus, *Child of the Dark*, p. 37.

36. Ibid., p. 131.

37. Cf. Daniel W. Patterson, *The Shaker Spiritual* (Princeton: Princeton University Press, 1979), p. 373.

38. Robert M. Levine, *Historical Dictionary of Brazil* (Metuchen, N.J., and London: The Scarecrow Press, 1979), p. 118.

39. Marx as quoted by Löwith, *Meaning in History* (Chicago and London: University of Chicago Press, 1949), p. 36.

40. A definition of the unconscious by Alfred Adler, I believe, but I haven't been able to locate it in his writings.

41. Joshua 23:14 and 3 Kings 2:2 in the Douay Version.

42. Walter de la Mare, *Ding Dong Bell* (New York: Knopf, 1924), pp. 77f.

43. Loren Eiseley commenting on de la Mare's story in *The Night Country*, p. 128.

44. John 8:28 ("I am" in the Greek rather than "I am he" as in the Revised Standard Version).

45. Exodus 3:14.

46. Herbert Mason, *The Death of Al-Hallaj* (Notre Dame, Ind., and London:

University of Notre Dame Press, 1979), pp. 21f.

47. Rouault, *Miserere*, Plate 9.

48. Rouault as quoted by Frank and Dorothy Getlein, *Georges Rouault's Miserere* (Milwaukee: Bruce, 1964), p. 25.

Notes to Chapter Four

1. John G. Neihardt, *Black Elk Speaks* (Lincoln: University of Nebraska Press, 1961), pp. 1f.

2. See chapter 3, note 15.

3. Immanuel Kant, *Critique of Pure Reason* trans. F. Max Muller (Garden City, N.Y.: Doubleday, 1966), p. 515.

4. Karl Marx and Friedrich Engels, *The Communist Manifesto* ed. Samuel H. Beer (New York: Appleton-Century-Crofts, 1955), p. 9.

5. W.B. Yeats, *A Vision* (New York: Collier, 1966), p. 144.

6. Neihardt, *Black Elk*, p. 29.

7. Leon Bloy, *The Woman Who Was Poor*, trans. I. J. Collins (New York: Sheed & Ward, 1947), p. 356 (the last sentence of the novel).

8. The title of Georgia O'Keefe's two paintings of a winding road that "goes downhill, then turns and sweeps and curves till it disappears in the hills below the mesa with the Sangre de Cristo mountains on beyond," *Georgia O'Keefe* (New York: Viking, 1976), plate 104.

9. Franz Kafka, "Reflections on Sin, Pain, Hope and the True Way" in *The Great Wall of China* trans. Willa and Edwin Muir (New York: Schocken, 1946), p. 279.

10. William Carlos Williams, *Autobiography* (New York: Random House, 1951), p. xi.

11. William Vaughn Moody, "The Death of Eve," in *The Poems and Plays of William Vaughn Moody* (Boston and New York: Houghton Mifflin, 1912), vol. 1, p. 409.

12. Ibid., p. 398.

13. Ibid., p. 409.

14. Flannery O'Connor, *The Complete Stories* (New York: Farrar, Straus & Giroux, 1971), p. 292.

15. Moody, *Poems and Plays*, vol. 1, pp. 133ff.

16. Ibid., p. 441.

17. Bloy, *The Woman Who Was Poor*, pp. 32f.

18. Ibid., pp. 343f.

19. Ibid., p. 355.

20. Ibid., p. 346.

21. Ibid., pp. 118, 217, and 355.
22. Ibid., p. 118.
23. Ibid., p. 217 (John 12:8).
24. See chapter 3, note 20.
25. Karl Marx, *Theses on Feuerbach*, Thesis 8 in Marx and Engels, *Basic Writings on Politics and Philosophy*, ed. Lewis S. Feuer (Garden City, N.Y.: Doubleday, 1959), p. 245.
26. C. S. Lewis, *Surprised by Joy* (London: Geoffrey Bles, 1955), pp. 23f.
27. Cf. Frank and Dorothy Getlein, *George Rouault's Miserere* (Milwaukee: Bruce, 1964), pp. 11ff.
28. Cf. Soren Kierkegaard's definition of faith as "the objective uncertainty due to the repulsion of the absurd held fast by the passion of inwardness" in *Concluding Unscientific Postscript*, trans. David Swenson and Walter Lowrie (Princeton: Princeton University Press, 1941), p. 540.
29. Dag Hammarskjold, *Markings*, trans. Leif Sjorberg and W. H. Auden (New York: Knopf, 1964), p. 66.
30. Katherine Anne Porter, *Ship of Fools* (Boston: Little Brown & Co., 1962), p. vii.
31. Leon Bloy, *Pilgrim of the Absolute* ed. Raissa Maritain, trans. John Coleman and Harry Lorin Binsse (New York: Pantheon, 1947), p. 45.
32. Herbert Mason, *The Death of Al-Hallaj* (Notre Dame, Ind. and London: University of Notre Dame Press, 1979), p. 30.
33. Simone Weil, *Waiting for God*, trans. Emma Crawford (New York: Putnam, 1951), p. 67.
34. Karl Marx, *Critique of Hegel's Philosophy of Right*, ed. Joseph O'Malley (Cambridge: Cambridge University Press, 1970), p. 131.
35. Ruth 1:16.
36. Walter de la Mare, *Ding Dong Bell* (New York: Knopf, 1924), pp. 77f.
37. Philippians 1:7.
38. Bloy, *The Woman Who Was Poor*, p. 217.
39. Flannery O'Connor, "Introduction to A Memoir of Mary Ann" in *Mystery and Manners* ed. Sally and Robert Fitzgerald (New York: Farrar, Straus & Giroux, 1969), p. 226.
40. Pierre Teilhard de Chardin, *The Divine Milieu* ed. Bernard Wall (New York: Harper & Row, 1965), p. 56.
41. I used this image in *A Search for God in Time and Memory* (New York: Macmillan, 1969), p. 119, to get at the way of the personal journey. Here I am using it to get from the particular way to the convergence of ways.
42. The letter is translated in Teilhard de Chardin, *The Divine Milieu*, p. 39.
43. Michael Polanyi, *Personal Knowledge* (New York: Harper Torchbooks, 1964), p. x.

44. Bloy, *The Woman Who Was Poor*, p. 345 (cf. pp. 346f. on hellfire and pp. 350f. on the woman going through fire; also p. 33, "when you are in the midst of the flames").
45. Neihardt, *Black Elk*, p. 2.
46. J.R.R. Tolkien, *The Lord of the Rings*, one-volume edition (London: George Allen & Unwin, 1969), p. 1122 (appendix B).
47. This is the opening scene in Ray Bradbury's novel *Dandelion Wine* (New York: Bantam, 1969), pp. 1–2.
48. Pierre Teilhard de Chardin, *The Mass on the World* in *Hymn of the Universe* trans. Gerald Vann (New York: Harper & Row, 1972), p. 16.
49. 2 Peter 1:19. I am taking this to refer to the vision described in verse 18 rather than to "the prophetic word" mentioned in verse 19 itself.

Notes to Chapter Five

1. Richard Collier, *The River that God Forgot: The Story of the Amazon Rubber Boom* (New York: Dutton, 1968).
2. I used this insight in *The Way of All the Earth* (New York: Macmillan, 1972), pp. 86ff. and then in *The Reasons of the Heart* (New York: Macmillan, 1978), pp. 20ff.
3. Cf. Jacques Maritain, *Neuf lecons sur les notions premieres de la philosophie morale* (Paris: P. Tequi, 1951), p. 176 ("La faute morale atteint l'incréé, nullement en lui-meme, il est absolument invulnérable, mais dans les choses, les effets qu'il veut et qu'il aime. Là, on peut dire que Dieu est le plus vulnérable des êtres").
4. Elie Wiesel, *Night*, trans. Stella Rodway (New York: Avon, 1969), p. 76.
5. Plato, *Gorgias* 469 in *The Dialogues of Plato*, trans. Benjamin Jowett (New York: Random House, 1937), vol. 1, p. 528. ("Then would you rather suffer than do injustice?" "I should not like either, but if I must choose between them, I would rather suffer than do.")
6. Rainer Maria Rilke, *Stories of God*, trans. M.D. Herter Morton (New York: Norton, 1963), p. 88.
7. Albert Camus, *The Myth of Sisyphus*, trans. Justin O'Brien (New York: Vintage, 1955), p. 91.
8. Gabriel Garcia Marquez, *One Hundred Years of Solitude*, trans. Gregory Rabassa (New York: Harper & Row, 1970), p. 254.
9. Collier, *The River*, under photograph of the High Life following p. 64. See ibid., p. 220 on each ton of latex costing seven lives.
10. Cf. Ypiranga's article cited in chapter 2, note 5. There Ypiranga mentions also that Antonio called his cabaret the High Life (in English).

11. Cf. chapter 2, note 5.
12. Plato, *Phaedrus* 230, *The Dialogues*, p. 236.
13. Fyodor Dostoevsky, *The Brothers Karamazov*, trans. Constance Garnett (London: Heinemann, 1955), p. 692.
14. Soren Kierkegaard, *Concluding Unscientific Postscript*, trans. David Swenson and Walter Lowrie (Princeton: Princeton University Press, 1941), p. 143. Cf. ibid., pp. 386ff. on suffering as "the essential expression for existential pathos."
15. Carl Gustav Jung, *Memories, Dreams, Reflections*, ed. Aniela Jaffe and trans. Richard and Clara Winston (New York: Vintage, 1963), p. 215.
16. Leon Bloy, *The Woman Who Was Poor*, trans. I. J. Collins (New York: Sheed and Ward, 1947), p. 217.
17. Eckhart, ed. and trans. Raymond B. Blakney in *Meister Eckhart* (New York: Harper & Row, 1941), p. 228.
18. Nikos Kazantzakis, *Zorba the Greek*, trans. Carl Wildman (New York: Simon & Schuster, 1952), p. 105.
19. Cf. Karl Marx, *Theses on Feuerbach*, Thesis 4 in Karl Marx and Friedrich Engels, *Basic Writings on Politics and Philosophy*, ed. Lewis S. Feuer (Garden City, N.Y.: Doubleday, 1959), p. 244.
20. Dag Hammarskjold, *Markings*, trans. Leif Sjoberg and W.H. Auden (New York: Knopf, 1964), p. 90.
21. W.B. Yeats, *A Vision* (New York: Collier, 1966), p. 181.
22. Herbert Mason, *The Death of Al-Hallaj* (Notre Dame, Ind. and London: University of Notre Dame Press, 1979), p. 12.
23. Archibald MacLeish, *J.B. A Play in Verse* (Boston: Houghton Mifflin, 1958), p. 14.
24. Ibid., p. 153.
25. Aquinas, *Summa Theologiae*, 1, q. 48, a. 6 (my translation). I am using the Marietti edition (Rome and Turin, 1950).
26. Georges Rouault, *Miserere*, (Boston: Boston Book and Art Shop with Trianon Press, 1963) Plate 35. Pascal, *Pensees*, 736 (my translation) (numbering according to the Pleiade edition, Paris, 1954).
27. John 3:16.
28. Christopher Smart, *Jubilate Agno*, Fragment A41 and B246, 248, 249 in Karina Williamson ed., *The Poetical Works of Christopher Smart*, vol. 1 (Oxford: Clarendon, 1980), pp. 4 and 53. Benjamin Britten put these words to music in *Rejoice in the Lamb*, op. 30 (composed for the consecration of St. Matthew's Church in Northampton, September 21, 1943).
29. Isak Dinesen [Karen Blixen], as quoted by Hannah Arendt in *The Human Condition* (Garden City, N.Y.: Doubleday, 1959), p. 155.
30. Isak Dinesen [Karen Blixen], *Last Tales* (New York: Random House, 1957), p. 26.

31. Cf. chapter 2, note 5.
32. Augustine, *Soliloquies*, Book 2, ch. 1, ed. Thomas F. Gilligan (New York: Cosmopolitan Science & Art Service, Co., 1943), p. 70 ("noverim me, noverim te") (my translation).
33. I saw the statue when visiting Mario Ypriranga who has it at his home in Manaus.
34. Kierkegaard, *Concluding Unscientific Postscript*, p. 401, footnote.
35. Ibid., p. 159.
36. Arendt, *The Human Condition*, p. 219.
37. Here I am going from Luke (6:20ff.) to Matthew (5:3ff) on the beatitudes (though the outcast in Luke too are cast out "on account of the Son of man").
38. Yeats, *A Vision*, p. 117.
39. "By relating itself to its own self and by willing to be itself the self is grounded transparently in the Power which posited it" in Soren Kierkegaard, *The Sickness unto Death*, trans. Walter Lowrie (London: Oxford University Press, 1941), p. 19.
40. A question posed by Leibniz and taken up by Heidegger as "the fundamental question of metaphysics." Cf. Martin Heidegger, *Introduction to Metaphysics*, trans. Ralph Manheim (Garden City, N.Y.: Doubleday, 1961), pp. 1ff, and "The Way Back into the Ground of Metaphysics," trans. Walter Kaufmann in *Existentialism from Dostoevsky to Sartre* (Cleveland and New York: Meridian, 1956), pp. 219ff.
41. Eckhart, p. 228.
42. Ludwig Wittgenstein, *Tractatus Logico-Philosophicus*, 6.44, ed. D. F. Pears and B. F. McGuinness (London: Routledge & Kegan Paul, 1961), p. 148 (my translation).
43. Smart, *Jubilate Agno*, Fragment A41, p. 4.
44. Genesis 1:10, 12, 18, 21, 25, and 31.
45. Soren Kierkegaard, "The Individual" in *The Point of View for My Work as an Author*, trans. Walter Lowrie (New York: Harper & Row, 1962), p. 129.
46. *Quarto de Despejo* is the diary that is translated under the title *Child of the Dark* (cf. chapter 3, note 7). *Casa de Alvenaria* (Rio de Janeiro: P. de Azevedo, 1961) has not been translated.
47. See chapter 3, note 20.
48. Aquinas, *Summa Theologiae*, 1–2, q. 113, a. 10 (I am taking the sentence "anima capax est Dei" out of the longer sentence "naturaliter anima est gratiae capax; *eo enim ipso quod facta est ad imaginem Dei, capax est Dei per gratiam*"—the part in italics is from Augustine, *De Trinitate*, 14, c. 8, in Migne's *Patrologia Latina*, vol. 42, p. 1044).
49. Here I am putting Aristotle's definition of God in terms of knowledge

(in *Metaphysics* 1074b 34) side by side with Dante's in terms of love (in the last line of *The Divine Comedy*).

50. Kierkegaard, *Concluding Unscientific Postscript*, p. 143.

51. *The Poems of George Herbert* (London: Oxford University Press, 1961), p. 180 (I have modernized the spelling). Ralph Vaughan Williams put this poem to music in "Five Mystical Songs" (September 14, 1911).

52. 1 Kings 9:3.

53. Aquinas, *De Veritate*, q. 1, a. 2 (my translation). (I am using the Marietti edition, Rome and Turin, 1949.) The circle for Aquinas is from "the thing outside the soul" to "intellect" to "appetite" and back to "the thing."

54. Daniel 9:23 ("a man of desires" in the Douay, and "greatly beloved" in the Authorized and the Revised Standard Version). No doubt, "greatly beloved" is the correct translation, but the contrast of the two is helpful here.

55. Yeats, *A Vision*, p. 136.

56. Picasso, *La Ronde*, July 25, 1961.

57. Aquinas, *Summa Theologiae*, 1, q. 14, a. 1 ("Anima est quodammodo omnia"). Aquinas cites this sentence from Aristotle (*De Anima* 431b 21) very often in discussions of soul, of intellect, and of will. Cf. my interpretation of these ideas in my article "St. Thomas' Theology of Participation" in *Theological Studies*, vol. 18, no. 4 (December, 1957), pp. 507ff.

58. Hammarskjold, *Markings*, p. 152 (Hammarskjold ascribes the idea here to St.-John Perse).

59. Michael Polanyi, *Personal Knowledge* (New York: Harper Torchbooks, 1964), p. x.

60. Cf. F.W. Nietzsche's story of "the ugliest man" in *Thus Spake Zarathustra*, trans. Walter Kaufmann in *The Portable Nietzsche* (New York: Viking, 1954), pp. 375ff., and my discussion of it in *The Reasons of the Heart* (New York: Macmillan, 1978), pp. 40, 46, and 53f.

61. Cf. Paul Tillich, *Christianity and the Encounter of the World Religions* (New York: Columbia University Press, 1963), pp. 70ff. (here he contrasts love and compassion but does not mention "judgment," though the term is a central one in the chapters preceding and following).

62. Plato, *Sophist* 251d, in *The Dialogues of Plato*, trans. Benjamin Jowett (New York: Random House, 1937), vol. 2, p. 260. On the five archetypes here cf. my *City of the Gods* (New York: Macmillan, 1965), p. 102, and on the idea of participation cf. my article cited in note 57.

63. I am alluding here to Aristotle's idea of a catharsis of pity and terror in his *Poetics*, 1449b 25 ff. That the pity is for the other and the fear for oneself cf. his *Rhetoric*, 1382b 26 and 1386a 26.

64. Cf. how "I know you" and "I am with you" go together in Exodus 33:12ff.

Notes to Chapter Six

1. Cf. Sigmund Freud, *Beyond the Pleasure Principle* trans. James Strachey (New York: Bantam, 1959), pp. 54f. on his idea that there is no time in the unconscious.
2. Leo Tolstoy, *War and Peace* trans. Louise and Aylmer Maude (New York: Simon & Schuster, 1970), p. 301.
3. Ingmar Bergman, "The Seventh Seal" in *Four Screenplays of Ingmar Bergman* trans. Lars Malmstrom and David Kushner (New York: Simon & Schuster, 1960), p. 138.
4. Edwin Abbott, *Flatland* (London: Seeley, 1884).
5. Karl Marx, *Theses on Feuerbach*, Thesis 6 in Karl Marx and Friedrich Engels, *Basic Writings on Politics and Philosophy*, ed. Lewis S. Feuer (Garden City, N.Y.: Doubleday, 1959), p. 244.
6. My conclusion in chapter 1. Cf. Aquinas cited in chapter 1, note 33.
7. E.g., the formulation at the Second Council of Constantinople in Henricus Denziger, *Enchiridion Symbolorum* (Barcelona: Herder, 1948), p. 98 (par. 213).
8. Joseph Conrad, *Heart of Darkness* (New York: Penguin, 1978), p. 39.
9. Karl Marx, *Critique of Hegel's Philosophy of Right*, ed. Joseph O'Malley (Cambridge: Cambridge University Press, 1970), p. 131.
10. My conclusion in chapter 2.
11. Cf. G.W.F. Hegel, *Phenomenology of Mind*, trans. James Baillie (New York: Macmillan, 1961), p. 237.
12. Cf. Ralph Ellison's prologue to his novel *Invisible Man* (New York: Random House, 1952).
13. Cf. the titles of her diaries cited in chapter 5, note 46.
14. My conclusion in chapter 3.
15. Dante, *Paradiso* 33:145 (the last line of *The Divine Comedy*).
16. My conclusion in chapter 4.
17. *The Poems of George Herbert* (London: Oxford University Press, 1961), p. 180.
18. Plato, *Sophist* 251d in *The Dialogues of Plato*, trans. Benjamin Jowett (New York: Random House, 1937), vol. 2, p. 260.
19. Deuteronomy 6:5.
20. Mark 12:30. Cf. Luke 10:27 and Matthew 22:37.
21. Cf. Jacques Maritain cited in chapter 5, note 3.

22. My conclusion in chapter 5.

23. 1 Kings 9:3.

24. Cf. Henryk Sienkiewicz, *Quo Vadis?* trans. Jeremiah Curtin (New York: The Heritage Press, 1960), chapter 69, pp. 499ff.

25. Aeschylus, *Agamemnon*, trans. Edith Hamilton *Three Greek Plays* (New York: Norton, 1937), p. 170.

26. Dag Hammarskjold, "A Room of Quiet: The United Nations Meditation Room," reprinted in Dag Hammarskjold, *Servant of Peace*, ed. Wilder Foote (London: The Bodley Head, 1970), p. 161.

INDEX